TOUGH
MANAGEMENT

The 7 Ways to Make
Tough Decisions Easier,
Deliver the Numbers,
and Grow Business in
Good Times and Bad

CHUCK MARTIN

McGraw-Hill

New York   Chicago   San Francisco   Lisbon   London   Madrid   Mexico City
Milan   New Delhi   San Juan   Seoul   Singapore   Sydney   Toronto

1 2 3 4 5 6 7 8 9 0   DOC/DOC   0 9 8 7 6 5

ISBN 0-07-145234-6

McGraw-Hill books are available at special quantity discounts to use as premiums and sales promotions, or for use in corporate training programs. For more information, please write to the Director of Special Sales, Professional Publishing, McGraw-Hill, Two Penn Plaza, New York, NY 10121-2298. Or contact your local bookstore.

This book is printed on acid-free paper.

TOUGH
MANAGEMENT

Other Books by Chuck Martin

The Digital Estate
Max E-Marketing in the Net Future
Net Future

The business world today is tougher than it's ever been, providing a challenging environment to all:

- Over the past few years, workload has increased for 80 percent of executives and managers, and significantly increased for almost half of them.
- Compensation has not increased significantly for 90 percent of executives and managers.
- The workplace of today is highly stressed, with 80 percent of executives and managers saying they are stressed, with almost a third feeling highly stressed. The reasons, in order, are budget constraints, deadlines, customer demands, and the number of hours worked.
- The amount of time executives and managers plan to stay with their organizations is changing, with the majority now planning to stay years rather than decades. The social contract between employer and employee has disappeared, thanks to actions by both parties.
- While 95 percent of executives and managers keep a list of things to do during the workday, 99 percent of them do not complete the tasks on those lists.
- Businesspeople today see keeping overall perspective as one of the most important skills to succeed, with more than two-thirds of them saying it is the most important skill for them to be successful today and in the future.

Together, factors such as these require managers to practice tough management. With tough management, workers constantly know where they stand, the focus on results is relentless, productivity increases, and customers ultimately receive better service.

The Seven Rules of Tough Management

There are seven distinct components, or "rules," that comprise tough management. Following these guidelines will help the over-

INTRODUCTION

Work today is more demanding than ever before. The world of work is forever changed, with no signs that it will ever go back to the way it was.

The bottom-line orientation required for budget-constrained organizations is the new way of life. The forever-increasing need for output without a proportionate increase in personnel is driving shareholders, executives, and managers to demand more from those who work for them, as well as from themselves.

Everyone is affected, as the burden falls on you, the people you manage, the people who manage you, your customers, their customers, and the employees and managers at all those places. Everyone is in the same situation with the work mantra of today: Do More with Less. People throughout the ranks are getting worn down, and it involves everyone.

Getting recharged and tackling tough decisions in these tough times requires a new, hardened approach by managers, with an eye toward pragmatically achieving results. Everyone in businesses of all types and sizes faces this new reality: the requirement to do more with less, deliver more, increase more without a total emotional drain. These tough times demand tough management.

Tough management is a way to approach work. It is a practical, reasonable, and organized way to get to decisions more easily, make the numbers on a consistent basis, have those around you understand where you stand, and increase the business.

ACKNOWLEDGMENTS

On behalf of myself and NFI Research, I would like to sincerely thank all of our members who take the time every two weeks to answer our surveys and provide us with candid feedback about what is happening in their business lives. These senior executives and managers are the knowledge engine underlying many of the points in this book.

We also want to thank all those business leaders who spent precious time with us to explain and detail their practical strategies and tips on how they are succeeding today. Their lessons are shared throughout the book.

Thank you to Philip Ruppel and Mary Glenn, my longtime friends at McGraw-Hill, who are always looking for the truth behind where business is headed and have a true appreciation for thoughtful and innovative insights and approaches.

Thanks to the great agents of the Leigh Speakers Bureau, who send me around the globe to speak at meetings of companies and customers to help them understand what they must do to succeed today and tomorrow.

Most important, I want to thank my family for their continual encouragement and loving understanding of what I do. To my wife, Teri, and my sons, Ryan and Chase, thank you for always being there. It matters more than anything else.

CONTENTS

To Teri

worked manager of today make tough decisions more easily, deliver the numbers that every organization is looking for, and grow the business.

1. ***Communicate clearly.*** Though many senior executives and managers feel they communicate well, the message does not get through. Tough management requires an abundance of communication that is clear, concise, timely, and truthful. Clear communication that is clearly received aligns those creating strategy with those executing throughout the ranks.

2. ***Force the hard decisions.*** Making the hard decisions when they need to be made at work is tough. The majority of executives and managers say their superiors do not deal with tough decisions right away. Managers need to collect all the necessary information available at the time, make the decision, communicate it, and then move on. The toughest decisions involve people, but they still have to be dealt with in a timely matter. Forcing the hard decisions also requires forcing office politics out of the equation.

3. ***Focus on results.*** Tough management requires that every person identify exactly the results that matter most at any given time and determine actions that produce those results. This requires focus, working smarter and harder, increasing productivity, and delegating. It also means being more realistic about what results are being demanded—whether you're the one doing the demanding or the one being demanded to execute—and assuring that both parties agree on the necessary tools and time frame needed to deliver those results.

4. ***Remain flexible.*** Managers today need to be organized so they can change directions quickly to keep pace with the changing needs of their organization and customers. Executives and managers are under increasing stress at work, especially because there is more to do than there is time to do it. Tough management requires pushing back and saying no at times, as well as "morphing" to be flexible. It also requires stopping something, such as institutionalized tasks, projects, or meetings, at work

and viewing yourself as more of a "virtual enterprise." Flexibility can help managers deal with changing employee loyalty.

5. *Prove your value to the company.* It is essential that you align with your company's values so that you can prove your value inside the enterprise. This means accepting even more new challenges and becoming the person everyone turns to for solutions. However, there is a fine line between proving your value and having the organization take advantage of you. Working away from the office and using commuting time can help you focus more on what you deliver rather than on number of hours worked.

6. *Force collaboration.* Tough management requires teamwork at every level. You can force collaboration by mapping vision statements specifically to members of the management team, with integrated results. This requires new levels of information sharing and a new willingness to learn.

7. *Practice tough management without being a tough guy.* You can deliver quantitative results without being brutal to subordinates in the process. Tough management requires executives and managers to pause at work, since workload and hours worked are getting out of control, potentially causing lost perspective. It means breaking away, improving employee morale, and taking steps to protect the talent. It also involves recognizing people for doing a good job and providing what is necessary for them to do their jobs better.

This book is supported by exclusive, primary research conducted over a period of more than a year by NFI Research, which I head. (See page xvii for details of the research.) I also interviewed many senior executives and managers, who candidly describe their best practices and ideas—and even frustrations—in this book. Except where specifically noted, the information in the book is based on our primary research or personal interviews.

This book is intended for managers at all levels of companies of any size. It is not intended to be the magic bullet to solve all of today's problems at work. However, it is intended to provide some help, a bit of assistance as you try to figure how to deal with (and sometimes even get off of) the treadmill of work, which keeps increasing in speed and intensity. The lessons in the book are not at the ten-thousand-foot level; they are down on the street. It is also intended to allow you to benchmark yourself against the viewpoints of other senior executives and managers on a host of workplace and business issues. This is not meant to be a grand business theory book about how things might work conceptually, but rather a pragmatic look at the way work really is today, down in the trenches.

We hope it provides each reader with something practical to take away, whether that be some thoughts on how to communicate better, be more flexible, be more demanding, or even loosen up a bit. We also hope it provides you with insight into what executives and managers are truly facing today, so that you can see where you fit in that context. Our intent in writing this book is to help you, even if only a little, as you succeed in these tough times, which is what tough management is all about.

About NFI Research and the Surveys

NFI Research is a U.S.-based research organization that has surveyed more than two thousand senior executives and managers globally every two weeks for five years. It has chronicled the transformation of business and countless workplace issues. I started the company as a way to keep in touch with executives and managers I have addressed in lectures throughout the world.

Every two weeks, NFI Research sends surveys via e-mail to two thousand senior executives and managers in fifty countries. The surveys are short, and results are totally anonymous. When the questions list potential answers, the directions generally ask respondents to check all answers that apply, thereby providing a majority consensus in results. The surveys do not necessarily match intensity of feeling about any given subject, but rather a sense of what the majority of senior executives and managers agree and disagree on. Some surveys are repeated over the years, so that benchmarking is possible and changes in attitude can be identified.

NFI does not share the e-mail addresses or any personal information about any of its members, who all have been invited by myself to join the members and participate in the surveys. There is no charge for membership, and the members all receive the survey results every other week for free. Response rates are always at least 10 percent. Survey participants fall into one of two categories: senior executive (CEO, chairman, president, senior vice president, general manager, etc.) or manager (assistant vice president, director, manager, supervisor, etc.). Respondents are generally about half senior executives and half managers.

Respondents also identify themselves by company size, based on total number of employees, and the results generally are a fair split among the groups. Some of those differences, as well as those between senior executives and managers, are used in the book when there are differences worth noting. A small sampling of the more than one thousand companies for which members work are Cendant, IBM, GE, Morgan Stanley, Merck, 3M, Microsoft, Texas Society of CPAs, CIGNA, Plus One, Fidelity, First Tennessee, Cabot Oil & Gas, Motorola, Borders, Ikon, Avantel, First Union, Bard Medical, American Express, Freddie Mac, Progressive, Travelers, American Gas, Heineken, Sandy Spring Bank, Snell Acoustics, Bank of America, Georgia Transmission, AT&T, California Credit Union, Continental Airlines, MasterCard, The Hartford, SAP, Pulte Home Corporation, and Exel Singapore.

Respondents also are asked to write additional comments, which many do, and many of those have been included in the book. Further information may be obtained at www.nfiresearch.com, where, if you are a senior executive or manager, you may apply for free membership. You may also contact me directly at chuck@nfire search.com.

TOUGH
MANAGEMENT

CHAPTER 1

COMMUNICATE CLEARLY

Communication is king in business. However, it is much like communicating with children. You state your point in a way that you consider to be very clear and obvious to the listener while the listener hears something totally different. Listeners hear what they want or expect to hear or, even worse, interpret what they think you meant, as opposed to what you said. Tough management requires an obsessive attention to the effectiveness of all communication, including the what, when, how, and, most important, the why of what you are communicating. In addition, the frequency and tone of the communication are important.

In the noisy and fast-paced world of today, it is increasingly important for businesspeople to share ideas, discuss tasks, and clearly communicate vision and direction. The overwhelming majority (94 percent) of senior executives and managers rank "communicating well" as the most important skill for them to succeed today and tomorrow. "Effective, consistent communication is the key, because by so doing a leader can attract and retain the only sustainable competitive advantage there is: a focused, motivated, and committed workforce," says one senior executive at a small company. Says another, "Most important: convince people. Then plan, organize, and execute to reach goals aligned with the mission combined with a vision that considers all stakeholders."

It can be difficult to convince without the ability to communicate well. Communicating well, which starts at an early age, is obviously important all the way through school and into the business world.

Better communication also makes working with others easier. "A lot of executives/leaders are too political and think they collaborate, when they are either telling people what they want to hear or telling different things to different people," says one manager. "I see too many games being played, no true friendships or trust. The word *communication* means so many things to different people." If members of a department or business team communicate well, much can be accomplished. Specific tasks become clear, and each member understands his or her role. When strategy and direction are clearly communicated, subordinates understand what they have to do.

Of course, communication is not the only skill required for success in business. The top skills after communicating well are, in order, the ability to stay focused, collaborate with others, keep overall perspective, and learn and prioritize tasks, as we discuss later in the book. "The success of the future will be integrating, communicating, and focusing personally and collaboratively," says one manager. "That will allow managers to need less fundamental expertise and be able to more effectively rely on their workforce." Another manager observes, "Since the late nineties, I feel baffled by what it takes to be a successful executive. On one hand, you have the visionaries, who seem to be swept out of office. On the other, you have the shortsighted being brought in. These shortsighted managers are driven primarily by a steadfast bureaucratic approach to issues. 'Tell me what you want, and I'll do it' is their attitude." No matter which skills you feel you have mastered, from staying focused to prioritizing tasks, they could be wasted without strong communication.

Clarity of Communication

If communication is so important, why are so many businesspeople so bad at it? One source of this shortcoming is communication habits, or lack of habits, that can start very early. Though various forms of communication are taught starting in elementary school, much of it is never carried into work life. For example, students are taught writing in terms of creating a well-formed thesis. They are taught to create a topic sentence, setting the stage for what the particular communication will be about. Students then are taught to create a thesis, or argument, which might contain several points. This is the argument from which following statements are used to support and elaborate. But students don't face the harsh realities of the business world, with internal politics, bottom-line focus, and stakeholder demands.

For many in business, communicating well comes naturally; for others, it does not. By the time people reach the management level, it is assumed they can communicate, both in writing and orally. Unfortunately, not all those receiving the message agree that it is coming through loud and clear. Tough management requires not only clarity in communication, but also increased frequency and checks for effectiveness.

To make sure communications at his organization are clear and understood by all, Barry Forbes, CEO of Westminster Savings in New Westminster, British Columbia, invites twenty-five of his employees to lunch every other month. No managers attend, and the employees are invited to ask any questions they wish. "It gets very interesting," says Forbes. "A six-month customer service teller asked me if I had a management succession plan."

"I ask them what we should change to make their jobs easier, and I always follow up, no matter what the issue," says Forbes, who has been CEO for twenty-six years. "I hand my card to every employee. The employees are the face to the members, not me. At the lunch meetings we discuss the 'why' of why we do things so that they can understand. They have my telephone number and e-mail address, and I encourage them to contact me." The credit union is the leader in its market and has less than 10 percent annual employee turnover, low for the industry.

How Well Do You Hear the Message?

Though communication is the most important skill for executives and managers, the majority of them are not clearly hearing directives from those above them. Ironically, those doing the communicating feel they are doing it very well. The overwhelming majority (92 percent) of senior executives and managers say they communicate well to their subordinates the roles of their daily, weekly, monthly, and quarterly projects and tasks in the context of their organization's long-term strategy and direction. However, only 59 percent of executives and managers say that their supervisors communicate those same roles to them either very or somewhat well, and only a quarter say very well.

"In general, executives are better at communicating downward than in hearing and understanding what their subordinates are trying to tell them through words, actions, and body language," says one manager. "There's a good reason why we have been designed with two ears, two eyes, and only one mouth."

Part of the difficulty in effective businesswide communication is the lack of time, as more people have their heads down trying to accomplish everything on their overloaded plates. Taking the time to truly communicate well sometimes often takes a backseat to the agenda of the day or the moment. "It is very difficult to communicate up and down the ladder," says a manager at a small company. "The lack of time is such a hindrance. It is interesting, though, how many senior executives communicate to a few of their staff but not all. It is almost like the first few of their subordinates they encounter are the fortunate few who hear the new plans, objectives, and projects." Says a senior executive at a small company, "Communicating up, down, and sideways is a daily task that takes energy and time. The time and effort invested keeps us all focused on our goals and is well worth it."

Part of the solution to the communication problem in the ranks is to understand how well you really do communicate. The real measure is how well your subordinates receive the communication.

After all, most people feel they communicate well, but a great number feel they do not *hear* well. Some executives realize that their communications do not always connect all they way down the ranks, so they take steps to allow others to help push their mes-

---

SURVEY: ORGANIZATIONAL COMMUNICATION

In general, how well does your supervisor communicate the roles of your daily, weekly, monthly, and quarterly projects and tasks in the context of your organization's long-term strategy and direction?

Very well	24%
Somewhat well	35%
Not very well	27%
Not at all well	11%

In general, how well do you communicate to your subordinates the roles of their daily, weekly, monthly, and quarterly projects and tasks in the context of your organization's long-term strategy and direction?

Very well	33%
Somewhat well	58%
Not very well	9%
Not at all well	0%

In general, how well does your supervisor communicate the roles of your daily, weekly, monthly, and quarterly projects and tasks in the context of your organization's long-term strategy and direction?

	Senior Executives	Managers
Very well	30%	19%
Somewhat well	33%	35%
Not very well	20%	34%
Not at all well	10%	12%

"This organization has a very clear understanding of who it is and, more important, who it is not. Makes for an easy communication of focus and direction on a daily, weekly, and monthly basis."

"This category is normally an area as supervisors we all could improve and coordinate with company long-term plans/goals."

"The biggest challenge in our firm is the lack of a consistent approach to strategy. The CEO changes weekly even though we put together a well-documented strategy plan. People start working on their plans to execute and deliver, only to have to stop and make changes as priorities change."

"Because my position is to increase sales for the company, it is not necessary to be told over and over what our goals are. Same with those who report to me; they are trained frequently on new techniques, but it is not a continuous type of communication in our line of business."

"As a corporate officer, I have a great view of the future needs of the corporation and share my insight appropriately."

"The funny thing about the communication issue, with regard to those above me, is that we are all on such a similar level of expertise that I am just allowed/expected to know and perform my specific job within the organization. Information does not always come to me or include me when it should. On the other hand, I am allowed to miss some very boring and mundane information sessions that only 'might' concern me."

"Toughest challenge is to communicate new strategies."

"Good, logical, and well-understood communication is vital for success in today's cluttered and 'overcommunicated' society."

"More and more in the organization at the top think of the long-term strategy while pressuring the field for short-term return. Communicating the long-term global picture might not be that relevant for this goal. In the current economy, long-term goals change often."

"Communication is too often limited to negative feedback when you do not correctly guess what your manager wants or have missed some impossible deadline your manager failed to question. Translation: your manager does not know what to do in every situation nor how to get something done in an unrealistic time frame. However, he or she does have the luxury of blaming you for failing to provide the solution."

sage along. "My boss is very vocal that he is not a great communicator and has delegated to me certain objectives that I overcommunicate," says a manager at a large company.

Another issue is being receptive to communication from superiors. "My best communication is with those on my team who seek the bigger picture," says one executive. "I struggle with those who want to be left alone to do their daily tasks. Getting people to peek over the walls of their short-term workload is one of my constant challenges."

Communicating tasks in the context of strategy starts at the top. "It is difficult to cast regular duties in terms of a corporate long-term strategy, when it has not been described well in the first place," says a manager at a medium-sized company. But once that has been accomplished, those who are communicating should check with their subordinates not on what was said, but on what was heard. Tough management requires more listening as part of the overall communication process, to determine what was heard compared with what was said.

Communicate, Communicate, Communicate

Tough management requires easy access to management and almost an overabundance of communication. It is rare that an executive or manager claims or complains that his or her organization has too much internal communication. Part of the secret of effective communication is to assure that everyone who needs to hear the message does, in fact, receive it in a timely fashion.

Joe Puglisi, Chief Information Officer (CIO) of EMCOR Group, one of the world's largest specialty construction firms, with twenty-six thousand employees in more than seventy subsidiaries and annual sales of about $4.6 billion, answers his own phone whenever he's in the office. People who work for him do the same, even though many have assistants.

"People can get to me easily, and I make sure I can get to my people whenever I need to," says Puglisi. The group uses e-mail, meetings, instant messages, and telephone all the time. Like many other managers in the United States, one of Puglisi's direct reports was totally opposed to using instant messaging because of the constant interruptions it causes. Puglisi got that manager to agree that in his case it would only be used between Puglisi and the manager, and the manager would not have to communicate with anyone else through IM.

"Our department, which is the core IT group, represents a well-connected group, even though it is spread across the country," says Puglisi. Although the corporate headquarters are in Norwalk, Connecticut, the IT group has managers based in Washington, Arizona, and New Jersey, and they all are in continual contact with Puglisi and each other. "We are better connected and coordinated than other departments." This takes a relentless communication among all involved, and EMCOR uses technology, such as online discussion groups, to support it. "I post a lot," says Puglisi, "and I drive people into the discussion areas."

When someone communicates directly to Puglisi and he thinks the information is relevant beyond him, he routinely has the subordinate electronically post the information internally for others to see and discuss. Puglisi monitors the discourse and dips in when necessary. For example, the director of support and training conducts a conference call every Friday with his staff, and when available, Puglisi sits in on the call.

"Two days ago, they were describing how the help desk was being reconfigured. I objected to the nomenclature being used. I had no problem with what they were doing, but rather how they were describing what they were doing. They were describing two teams, a distinction between one group and another support group. The point was they were supposed to be integrating the two groups."

It is watching and identifying this kind of subtlety that keeps the strategic thinking and intent in line with the tactics at the manager and employee level. EMCOR internally conducts many meetings and conferences, encourages frequent discussions, and hosts an annual summit of key managers.

As a communicator, Puglisi spends much of his time interacting in small groups as well as with all the EMCOR companies. "I talk to the presidents and the CEOs of the companies. We just renegotiated our telecommunications contracts, so we broadcast it to the companies to say they all can take advantage of it."

As in many large companies, the EMCOR subsidiaries are autonomous, which presents challenges to departments, such as IT, that cut across all parts of the company. For example, the IT group introduced to the company a plan to standardize use of Dell computers, to provide economies of scale in purchase, support, etc. "We brought the IT people to Dell in Austin. Some of them were empowered, so they bought in. Some others, their management preferred the cheap boxes they were buying. So at the management conference, we have to lay out the standardization case and show how and why it is good. You can't achieve the value unless volume buy-in occurs. You have to overcommunicate these things."

Tough management requires that communication be constant and in a continual loop. Peter Baker, who reports directly to Puglisi as the director of applications at EMCOR, is constantly in communication with his boss as well as his peers, customers, and vendors. His role is to manage all the outside applications and development contractors and vendors who do work for EMCOR. He sees a key part of this role as keeping the communication flowing bidirectionally.

"We're all straight up and down the line," says Baker. "If Joe tells me something that will impact a vendor, the information is passed on immediately. It makes good business sense. I either call or IM the vendor, and if it has to be formal, I'll send an e-mail. The vendors appreciate this, big time. We know how to manage vendors. A lot of times, they [the vendors] know more about EMCOR than some of the EMCOR companies themselves. We bring the vendors in at the corporate level, and they learn who EMCOR is and how the operating companies work together." Because of the constant communication, the vendors end up feeling like a part of EMCOR. Tough management requires this type of constant communication, as practiced at EMCOR. It involves easy accessibility and constant bidirectional communication.

Allowing the free, bidirectional flow of information in an organization or department is cultural. In the case of EMCOR, the open-communication stage was set at the top, by Puglisi, and the people who survive are those who fit the culture. This means that hoarding of information is not tolerated.

A side benefit of this free flow of information is that people can make correct decisions relatively quickly, since all stakeholders already are following the details and discussions leading up to a decision. "In our group, everyone has the information, so consensus is pretty quick," says Baker.

Tone of Communication

Just as there are many forms of communication, there are also various tones that can go along with the messages. Sometimes what is communicated has nothing to do with the actual words used. At other times, it could be a look, a perception, or a statement not made. In short, the tone of what is communicated can be as critical as the message.

- *Just the facts.* There is nothing flowery in this kind of communication, where only facts are stated, without context. The recipient gets the data, but not necessarily the relative importance. Each recipient gets to create his or her interpretation of the meaning and import.
- *Angry eyes.* The listener can tell by looking at your eyes that this message matters to the speaker big time. It is too easy to misinterpret that the speaker is angry about not getting that promotion while delivering a totally unrelated message to someone else.
- *Between the lines.* We hear what was said but know deep down that the speaker doesn't really mean that. Everyone knows the real meaning of an announcement that a "valued" member of the team is leaving the company to "pursue other interests." Translation? Fired.
- *Curt.* Maybe the boss doesn't buy in to this communication and is just following orders. A curt tone leaves the listener guessing.
- *Generic.* The generic tone describes the way the boss generally communicates. These messages usually contain nothing of note. They can be ignored like all the rest.
- *The big one.* This is the memo that talks about all you've been through together and the tough times coming during the next year. Translation? Dust off the résumé; a hit list is being made.
- *The joker.* Some messages contain so many genuinely funny comments that it's difficult to tell when the person is really not kidding.
- *Pals talk.* When messages always treat subordinates like buddies rather than subordinates, the communications don't always carry the necessary weight. It can be a shocking surprise when the really tough message has to be delivered.

Corporate Truth Versus Street Truth

The result of bad communication is a disconnection between strategy and execution. One of the toughest challenges businesses face today is how to bridge the gap between the top executive's vision and the reality of the managers and workers who must make that vision happen.

Managers and employees generally are closer on a day-to-day basis to customers and their short-term demands, needs, and expectations, which may not be the same as the demands, needs, and longer-term expectations of the corporate strategy. This gap can be the ultimate undoing of a leader's strategy, as well as total frustration in the ranks, as managers see a distance between what their leaders say and what their customers want. It is the difference between what I have previously labeled "corporate truth" and "street truth."

The *corporate truth* is what the chief executive or corporate leadership announces to the world, Wall Street, or even the company's own employees that the business is going to do. This often is based on self-perceived capabilities of the chief executive, who may think, "This is the best course for the company, and I believe I can pull this off." The *street truth* is the reality of the company's managers and employees, who hear the message and determine how much of that pronouncement actually will be realized. The middle manager might hear the corporate pronouncement and think, "What on earth is he thinking? Our customers don't want us to do that." The street truth is more closely aligned with the day-to-day realities of the managers and employees who do the work.

One of the primary reasons for this gap between corporate truth and street truth involves communication itself. The gap results when executives do not effectively communicate their messages to their subordinates, leaving managers to draw their own conclusions about details of company direction. Managers then behave according to their own understanding of how to act, based on other things, such as customer expectations, self-interest, and individual relationships.

The problem is particularly acute if the executives who are trying to deliver a message are perceived to be communicating only for show. For a message to be delivered, it must also be received, and skepticism about the purposes of the communication does not help people listen well.

In the case of EMCOR, CIO Puglisi identified this potential gap at the beginning of his tenure, more than five years ago. "The higher up you go, the closer you are to strategic thinking. In the trenches, it's how to get through the day," says Puglisi. "Skills are lacking in linking those things together. Senior management should appreciate that and keep the lines of communication open through the ranks." When he took over as CIO, Puglisi made sure that all lines of communication were not only open, but also regularly used.

When Puglisi is traveling and happens to be near one of EMCOR's many offices, he makes it a point to drop in for a visit. "They know I'm coming. I always ask to go to a job site. There's nothing like being in touch with the business of the business. I'm more interested in hearing from the manager what is his problem this week."

The Last Third

Staying in communication with the heads of the EMCOR companies as well as getting a firsthand look at the customer of the business allows Puglisi a perspective to appreciate the value of comprehensive communication. His advantage, which not all executives share, is that he was the first corporate CIO and had the opportunity to start the group with a policy of open and total communication.

However, there still is a tremendous downside to even the best communication efforts. It is what I call the *law of the last third*. This says that one-third of people hearing a logical communication will understand and buy in almost immediately. The second third will have some questions but ultimately can be convinced and will follow suit. It is the last third that presents enormous problems for companies of all sizes. It is this last third that just never buys in to anything, preferring to delay interminably or never do whatever is being requested. Reasons vary, from groups feeling that things are fine the way they are to their just not agreeing that someone else has a better way to do what that group is already doing.

For example, EMCOR's decision to standardize on Dell computers was negotiated and then announced companywide. About a third of the companies bought in almost immediately. The second third ultimately came along as well, once provided with additional communication for better understanding. But the last third still chose not to go along. When this occurs, a mandate from the top may be required, which is not efficient for all cases.

Many top managers have to continue communicating to build critical mass, ultimately making it easier for top management to get the message across.

The Worlds of Senior Executives and Managers

One of the reasons communications are not clearly translated within an organization is that senior executives and managers look at and live in somewhat different business worlds. Essentially, there is a difference in the viewpoints of senior executives and managers on a host of workplace and business issues. The differences are not necessarily negative, but they do reflect a somewhat differing view of parts of the business world and how each other functions on a day-to-day basis. For example, 38 percent of senior executives (CEO, chairman, president, senior vice president, general manager, etc.) say their workload has increased significantly compared with the load two years ago. Among managers (assistant vice president, director, manager, supervisor, etc.), 53 percent say their workload has increased significantly. So more managers than executives feel they have taken on more of the burden. They differ on other issues as well:

- *Toughest decisions.* The number one tough call for the majority of senior executives involves hiring and firing, while for managers, the toughest for the majority of them involves changing jobs.
- *Customer expectations.* While 30 percent of senior executives say that their customers' expectations now compared with two years ago are extremely higher, only 15 percent of managers say so.
- *Meeting customer expectations.* When asked whether their organization meets their customers' expectations, 42 percent of senior executives say it does, and 31 percent of managers say it does.
- *Commuting time.* Senior executives spend less time commuting to and from work. While 22 percent of senior executives spend one hour or more commuting, 47 percent of managers do. Both spend most of that time listening to the radio.
- *Challenge.* While 61 percent of senior executives say they are very challenged, just 43 percent of managers are. However, when asked if the people who report to them are very challenged, 60 percent of senior executives say yes, compared with 35 percent of managers.
- *Compensation.* Responding to questions about changes in their income, 14 percent of senior executives said their total compensation had increased significantly, while only 7 percent of managers said the same. However, 23 percent of senior executives reported that their total compensation had decreased, compared with 9 percent of managers.
- *Hours worked.* While 76 percent of senior executives work more than 50 hours a week, 52 percent of managers put in that much time.

Tough management requires understanding the context in which others live. Communication can be effective only when you understand the work-life context of those to whom you are communicating.

Communicating and Internal Forces

Tough management requires more attention to internal forces, such as attaining internal buy-in from all the managers and their troops. Narrowing the gap between what an executive pronounces and what a manager executes requires three important steps:

1. *Dramatically increase managers' knowledge and understanding of a company's direction.* The short-term decisions that dominate managers' lives must be clearly linked to the overall corporate vision—or at least not work against it. To delegate without increasing the distance between corporate truth and street truth, companies must enable managers to make decisions consistent with the corporate strategy, even without an executive staring over their shoulders.

2. *Expect and deliver measurable results.* The tough management moves linked to strategy must individually and collectively produce clearly demonstrable results that validate the vision and enable a CEO to demonstrate that the overall corporate direction is viable.

3. *Flow market information back.* The corporate strategy must incorporate flexibility and a constant flow of information as a priority, so that strategy is constantly in touch with new information and changing market conditions. This helps keep strategy and tactics connected, each with its own role but supporting and reinforcing the other.

Most often, both senior executives and managers want to do what is in the best interest of the organization and the shareholders. The challenge is one of interpretation, of how well the message is being communicated from the top and how well it is synchronized with the ever-changing realities and immediate tasks at the managerial level. Closing the communication gap between executives and managers can allow an organization to move forward in one direction, with strategy and execution together.

The 50 Percent Rule

With so much on the plate of every executive and manager, it is challenging to take the appropriate amount of time to communicate effectively. Communication traditionally has been viewed as communication from the one doing the communicating to the one receiving the communication. Therein lies the fundamental problem in today's work world. Rather than comprehensive interaction between boss and subordinate, there often is a dictate from the superior, which from that person's point of view, is a totally proper message. The irony is that the recipient often is closer to the subject about which the superior is making the decision, though the ultimate decision is effectively taken away from that person, once the superior feels he or she has enough information to dictate some form of issue resolution.

These communications can be shortsighted, temporarily solving an immediate problem while missing an opportunity to involve the recipient in the decision process.

When resolving an issue or problem, executives and managers should adhere to what I call the "50 percent rule." This means that more than half of the communication from the superior should involve listening, not talking.

John Nadeau is president of Chest PT [Physical Therapy] Services, a New England–based health care agency that deploys therapists to children with cystic fibrosis. Nadeau manages ninety-five therapists and spends much of his time "putting out fires," or solving problems, often between the therapist and the patient or family. However, much of the time Nadeau spends communicating with his therapists involves the president listening and the therapist talking:

> *Their job is so important and their skills so valuable, I see them*
> *as a precious commodity for the client, the cystic fibrosis patient.*
> *They're the independent professionals, and my job is to put out any*
> *fires. The whole point is that their job is to provide a professional*

service to their clients, so if they're going to serve any client, they're going to have to attempt to make it work for this one. This is difficult at times, because the clients are often quite ill and they may see the need for our service as a negative, that is, getting in the way of life. Especially teenaged patients.

The therapists deal with the same clients over a long period of time, and the personalities can get on each other's nerves from time to time, especially in the emotionally charged atmosphere concerning an ill child. I have to communicate that their skills are a precious commodity for their patient. You have to let them talk and you must really listen to what they're telling you. Many times, they come up with their own solution as they talk. They need someone to listen, and you support them in their decision. Clear communication means clearly listening. You have to hear from the therapist and client what the true problem is before a solution can be reached. Sometimes I need to be a conduit or a lightning rod for frustrations. But I'd rather the client be upset with the president of the company than the person they have to see every day. Sometimes it means communicating the bad news. The bad news for a client is that they are demanding a level of service that does not exist, such as we cannot be there at 2:00 A.M. or they are desperate for a cure that does not yet exist.

However, management also has to understand what's going right, not just what's going wrong. I learned this from my father many years ago. In the 1970s, bookbinding had changed. My father had been a bookbinder since when it was done by hand. In the seventies, the press where he worked installed a machine that they called a million-dollar line. They set it up with the printed pages going in one end, and the machine would make the book. It was a bookbinding machine that effectively replaced the assembly line method. My father worked the third shift, from 11:00 P.M. until 7:00 A.M. A few of what he called the "big bosses" wanted to know why he was able to make the machine produce more books than the other two shifts.

They came to talk to him, and his answer was pretty straightforward. He said the machine made more books for him because there were no big bosses around when he worked. They were puzzled by his answer. He told them that the other two shifts could do just as well, since they all had learned how to run the million-dollar machine. However, he told them that management would always want them to run the machine at a higher speed, since they were never satisfied with the current speed.

He told them that the high speeds would cause the books to jam, and clearing the jam would take a lot of time. My father ran the machine at slower speeds and had far fewer jams. The guys running the machines knew the machine's limitations, but the big bosses on the day shifts wouldn't listen.

So I treat the therapists as the professionals that they are. I trust that they know how to perform their job and that they will do it well. I only have issues with them when the professional standards aren't being met.

I never yell, and I'm never even stern. They know me as a very pleasant person. So to get my message across, I only have to be slightly less than pleasant. I tell the therapists they're awesome all the time, and I never write a memo without sincerely thanking them for their great service to our clients at the end of every letter. We still have the first therapist we ever hired.

You can get more from people by pulling it from them than you can from pushing demands onto them. Most people derive happiness from a job well done. That can be a powerful driving force in their daily work lives.

Effective, Truthful Communication

Communication from the top leaders of organizations appears, for the most part, to be frequent and consistent, but not totally truthful. However, before business leaders start to take any of their communication capabilities and effectiveness for granted, they should know that many in the management ranks see executive communication as not frequent enough, inconsistent, and full of messages that will likely make the leader look good:

- Sixty-two percent of senior executives and managers say the amount/frequency of communication from their top leaders to managers and employees is high.
- Only 17 percent rate that communication as "extremely high" in frequency and amount.
- Another 38 percent rate the amount/frequency of communication from above as either somewhat or extremely low.
- Regarding the messages, 59 percent say communication from their leaders is consistent.
- Another 22 percent says it is inconsistent.
- Almost half rate their leaders' communication as straightforward.

When it comes to communicating in a way that will likely make them look good, leaders are viewed by a fifth of executives and managers to be in that category. More startling, 93 percent of managers do not rank their leaders' communication as totally truthful. "Yesterday, the validity of the information was based on who was delivering it," says Gord Huston, president and CEO of Envision Credit Union in British Columbia. "It was command and control. Today and tomorrow it is the message itself that will be judged, not who is sending it. People have to be honest."

"My organization is reasonably good about the frequency of communications," says one manager at a large company. "However, the quality has much to be desired. Often the communications are much too long, and the main points are lost in the inundation of detail."

Everyone realizes that with so much to do these days, it is sometimes difficult to find the time to properly relay an effective message. "Communication is always a problem," says a senior executive at a small company. "Not that top leadership doesn't want to communicate or doesn't think it is important to communicate, but making the time is a real challenge." Says a senior executive at a medium company, "When communicated, the amount is high and

SURVEY: EFFECTIVE COMMUNICATION

From the top leaders of my organization, the amount/frequency of communication to managers and/or employees is:

Extremely high	17%
Somewhat high	44%
Somewhat low	30%
Extremely low	9%

In general, communication from the top leaders of my organization is:

Consistent	59%
Straightforward	48%
Customer-focused	41%
Not frequent enough	33%
Inconsistent	22%
What will likely make them look good	19%
What they think people want to hear	14%
Self-serving	13%
Totally truthful	13%
Convoluted	10%
More targeted toward Wall Street	8%
Selfless	5%
Too frequent	4%
Irrelevant	3%

From the top leaders of my organization, the amount/frequency of communication to managers and/or employees is:

	Senior Executives	Managers
Extremely high	26%	11%
Somewhat high	41%	48%

continued

	Senior Executives	Managers
Somewhat low	29%	30%
Extremely low	4%	12%

In general, communication from the top leaders of my organization is:

	Senior Executives	Managers
Consistent	64%	56%
Straightforward	55%	43%
Customer-focused	42%	41%
Not frequent enough	26%	38%
Inconsistent	20%	24%
Totally truthful	20%	7%
What will likely make them look good	16%	20%
What they think people want to hear	12%	15%
Self-serving	10%	15%
More targeted toward Wall Street	7%	9%
Convoluted	6%	14%
Selfless	4%	6%
Too frequent	4%	4%
Irrelevant	0%	6%

consistent and carefully worded; it's just not frequent enough. The difficulty is when to communicate things. If too early, inaccurate conclusions can be drawn. If too late, complaints surface about not being in the know."

True communication obviously means getting company information from more than just the top leaders. "To truly understand what is going on, communication with others in the organization is important," says one manager at a large company. At a medium-sized company, a manager observes, "Although in general the amount of communication is pretty high, the messages are not consistent enough. We need to do a better job of being on the same page with each other."

Not every organization has effective communicators at all levels, making it a challenge to get all the appropriate information to all the right people. "I am in constant communication with employees regarding sales matters for customers," says the vice president of sales at one organization. "Our president, however, is weak in his communications to the employees about corporate matters."

There are also what might be considered routine communications, such as "Here is the news of the recent reorganization" or "We all need to learn to do more with less" or the typical corporate motivational speech with self-congratulations for everyone.

Sometimes effective communication becomes the victim of expediency. Tough management requires that business leaders take the time to add to their messages, so that rather than just concentrating on getting the work done, more in the ranks understand the why and how to go about those tasks.

VOICES FROM THE FRONT LINES: EFFECTIVE COMMUNICATION

"Top management should practice what they preach, and that is not always the case."

"Companies today are concentrating on getting the work done and aren't communicating effectively the why and how to go about that task."

"Communication is becoming a greater problem. I do not believe it is intentional. I think that it is a victim of expediency. Also, top management does not appreciate the importance of frequent, honest, two-way dialogue in today's environment."

"We just completed a major acquisition, and just as we should be getting more frequent and clearer communication, our new CEO has gone somewhat underground. This, combined with a recent reduction in force, has left morale low at a critical time."

"Communication is key for our CEO, and he spends one day [per] month just visiting staff and talking—communicating with them (he wants to meet real people, not management, on his tours around the world)."

Tough management requires frequent and consistent communication. Once communications are fine-tuned so that messages are easily conveyed and well understood, decisions at the top can be understood all the way through the ranks. This also makes it easier to convey in a clear way when and why a tough decision has been made, which we discuss in the next chapter.

CHAPTER 2

FORCE THE HARD DECISIONS

Not all decisions in business are created equal. Since it is only natural to follow a path of least resistance, it's often less painful to deal with easier decisions and wait longer to tackle those that are more difficult or complex. Tough management requires the exact opposite: that executives and managers make the tough calls as soon as possible and encourage those around them to do the same and then move on. Making tough calls and forcing them throughout the business won't necessarily make you a lot of new friends, but it will create a new sense of respect for the decision-making process everywhere in the chain of command.

Putting Off the Tough Calls

Making the hard decisions at work can be tougher than it looks, especially the higher up the chain you go. A bad call can hurt not only the business but also one's personal career. While many managers feel their bosses defer the tough calls, the majority of them say they themselves deal with the difficult decisions immediately.

Sixty-two percent of executives and managers say they make the tough decision at work right away, and 58 percent get opinions from others first. For executives and managers personally:

- They feel they act in a timely fashion with enough input from relevant parties.
- Almost no one feels he or she avoids tough calls or makes them without enough thought.
- Ninety-five percent say they do not delegate the tough calls to others.
- About nine out of ten do not feel they focus on easier decisions.
- Almost nine out of ten do not feel they defer the tough calls.

However, senior executives and managers have a totally different viewpoint when it comes to how they see their superiors acting:

- Only a third believe their superiors deal with the tough decisions right away.
- About a third say their superiors seek others' opinions before making the tough calls.
- About a third say their superiors defer the tough decisions.
- Almost a third say their superiors wait until absolutely necessary to make the decisions.
- Almost nine out of ten do not feel their superiors focus on easier decisions.

So while individuals feel they are making the tough decisions right away, they feel their bosses are neither making them nor getting others' opinions first.

Time Frames for Tough Decisions

Timing and the amount of information play significant parts of making the difficult decisions. "How you deal with tough decisions depends on the immediacy required," says a senior executive at a small company. "Dealing with someone who is a thief and dealing with someone who might be a valuable partner require different time frames, though perhaps the same importance."

"Making a tough decision when I don't have enough knowledge or information is the hardest thing I have to do," says a manager at a large company. "Yet I have to make those decisions, and I do make them, using intuition, instinct, and anything else that helps. Sometimes people's careers and money are at stake, and a mistake can have huge consequences."

"Decisions are commonly made difficult because of a lack of adequate information," says a manager at a medium-sized company.

Holding off on making the ultimate decision can be a very tough call in itself. "Many executives mistake acting and being perceived as tough with making tough and fair decisions," says a senior executive at a large company. "Sometimes, deciding to be patient and objective is the toughest decision of all."

"Skillful inaction with difficult decisions has some value, but only to provide sufficient time to gather enough information to make an intelligent decision," says a senior executive at a large company.

"Whenever possible, leaders need to take enough time to study the possible consequences of a decision before acting," says a manager at a small company. "When a decision is made thoughtfully and then decisively, negative fallout can be mitigated."

Decisions often become more difficult higher in the ranks, because at that level, more people and potentially more of the business can be affected. However, that is not always the case, since managers at all levels are empowered at least enough to make some of the tough calls, which can have serious consequences. However, there are some tough decisions that can have dramatic professional and personal consequences, either positively or negatively.

When IBM identifies a potential sea change in a market, it creates what it calls an EBO, an emerging business organization, to analyze that market and determine what role, if any, IBM should play in it. For example, when the Internet and the World Wide Web were up and coming, the Armonk, New York–based company established an EBO and ultimately determined that the company should make a serious investment in e-business, which it ultimately did. The company also created EBOs for life sciences, grid computing, and more recently, the Linux computer operating system.

"We set up an EBO to execute our business strategy," says Doug Dreyer, worldwide program director of Linux strategy and business development at IBM. "Early on we felt open source would gain momentum and we needed to seize the opportunity, but timing was critical," says Dreyer.

Dreyer focused on the telecommunications industry globally and worked across IBM brands to build commercial off-the-shelf (COTS) technology for next-generation network solutions. Says Dreyer, "The network and the enterprise are converging. We made a tough decision to change the traditional legacy approach of using custom-engineered products and introduced off-the-shelf products based on standards. Since we had a relatively low share of the network server market, it made sense. We saw Linux and open standards as game-changing technologies, but it was a three- to five-year investment and sell cycle. The opportunity is significant, but open standards, Linux, and COTS needed to evolve together. . . . It was a gamble on timing."

IBM made the tough decision to enter the Linux market, and Dreyer had to make the tough decision whether to join the Linux group at IBM. At the time, he was successfully leading a sales organization in another area of IBM. When faced with whether to join the Linux strategy group at its beginnings several years ago, the result of taking a business chance on Linux was an unknown. If the EBO analyzed the market and found that it was not the right time to enter, Dreyer could find himself looking for "placement" somewhere else within the company. However, Irving Wladawsky-Berger, the same person who pushed for IBM to enter Internet and e-business markets in a big way, was advocating the group, and Dreyer trusted his vision and that he had done the right homework. Says Dreyer:

We had a task force look at this and saw a huge opportunity. We had an established leader who assembled the best minds across the company and concatenated their recommendations into a successful business case. Now it seems like an easy decision, but at the time it was a very bold move for IBM.

When you work directly with customers you can see the critical mass for change building. Four or five years ago Linux market adoption was very low, but I figured that Irving had a proven track record in identifying other emerging technologies. The Linux EBO had good people and corporate support, but it could have been a career move that ended up being dead-ended.

The very first company risk is the creation of the EBO itself. The corporate risk is that you could be stuck with a group of people that has deep knowledge of a technology that's not important . . . or it's too early to be commercialized.

The personal risk is taking the gamble that your company will be successful enough to keep funding the EBO. If it doesn't, or the timing is too early or too late, or if you don't perform well, there are a lot of places to get sidelined in the process.

If you're not working with customers and partners, you won't see the market inflection points and can't make the tough decision in time . . . or you'll make the wrong one. Tough decisions don't get made unless you have key high-level executives with industry knowledge outside the organization using their inside influence to effect change. One of the toughest decisions is realizing that you have to make one.

Ducks and Eagles

The big problem in making the hard decisions has much to do with the personal and professional well-being of the person making the call. After all, who wants to be perceived as the bad guy in tight market conditions where there is a family to support and mortgage payments to make? Therein lies a fundamental problem in why some decisions are not made soon enough: no one wants to make them. It's not that a decision cannot be made; it's that no one wants to step up and make it and be held accountable.

Terry Ransford is senior vice president of Northern Trust, a major regional bank headquartered in Chicago. As a relative newcomer in a somewhat fraternal organization, Ransford holds responsibilities that include overseeing products, systems, and trading. Like many executives, Ransford works ten hours a day in the office, as well as more at home, on weekends, and during lunch at his desk. But with less than five years at the bank, Ransford finds that hard decisions routinely and regularly bubble up to him.

"There are so many situations in which we try to please all constituencies," says Ransford. "At some point, all those worlds collide, and someone has to step in and make the tough decision."

He often finds himself to be that person, whether desired or not: "Hey, I'm always the guy there when people throw up their arms and say, 'What are we going to do?'"

A situation in which people are almost giving up in frustration presents a great opportunity for making the tough call:

- Every stakeholder has had his or her say.
- Everyone's position on the issue is clearly known.
- It is agreed that there is no resolution in the current situation.
- No one has made the tough call yet, or there wouldn't be a problem.

The opportunity here is for an objective outsider (the boss, a senior executive, even the CEO) to step in and moderate a quick resolution by a tough call. The first step is to make it clear to the participants that whatever they are coming up with is not working; otherwise, they would not all be frustrated. It also should be clear that they do not have the solution, so something different has to be called for.

More often than not, Ransford finds himself in that role. Says Ransford:

I tell them we have to step back and then get them to agree that there is no perfect solution and that the end game is more important than the things in the middle, so let's not take our eye off the ball. It's easier to not make any decisions, because if you don't do anything, you can't get into trouble, especially when things are tough. It's typical conflict avoidance. When the situation is tough enough, people are forced to make those decisions. The first thing to do is to quantify as much as you can and take the emotion out of it. Facts will neutralize the personalities as well.

Then you have to communicate the decision to those below. If they perceive the decision was for internal political reasons, that's bad and people resent it. The challenge is to make the best business decision without the politics. The perception is more dangerous than the decision. But if you have an analytical process, you can rationalize the decision. It might not be the right decision ultimately, but it was the best decision at the time, given all the circumstances.

There was a time that the auto industry was shipping jobs offshore and the U.S. was losing workers. But now Toyota is building plants in the U.S. and hiring those same people in America. Great companies get to the top, don't look inward, and fail. They don't reinvent themselves enough, and they tend to blame someone else.

When it comes to making the tough decisions, there are generally two types of managers, what I call the *ducks* and the *eagles*. The ducks tend to follow the lead duck, don't really make any waves, and certainly never take a chance to go out on their own to make a bold decision. That's OK, since every organization needs people who do work, even if they do not venture out of their assigned roles and tasks. The eagles are significantly more independent, tend to look at decisions in a broader context, and are not as risk-averse as the ducks. The ducks keep an organization running, once it is set up, while the eagles help determine the best ways to advance the organization.

"In every company there are the 'doers' and other employees," says Ransford. "It's the day-to-day block-and-tacklers versus the innovators." Everyone in a company looks to the innovators, or eagles, to make the tough decisions.

"For them, it's the thrill of doing something new," says Ransford. "Doers are motivated a different way; they are less concerned with protecting their own status. Maybe it's because of self-confidence. When the company has to make do with less, it will keep the doers, not the political straphangers."

Ransford had one situation concerning a part of the business that involved commissions to brokers, money managers, and large pension plans. There was a program that reallocated portions of commissions back to pension funds. After all client fees were paid, Northern Trust was barely covering the program's costs and, in some cases, losing money. The new accounts being sold were to very well-known, large corporations, which looked very appealing to Northern Trust. Ransford explains:

> We ended up in deals that didn't make economic sense. Corporately it looked good, but the math didn't work. So the decision was, Do you hurt your relationship with the broker on the street or lose the big clients? I had to get everyone in a room together and show that some of the business was being enrolled at negative revenue. It sounded good to say we won all this business, but the math didn't work over time.
>
> In the end, when you put all the players in one room, they get it. They hate it, but they get it. They see that the revenue is tied to their compensation and there will be no revenue, so they come around. People move on. They didn't talk to me for a week, and then they moved on.

Forcing the hard decisions requires three steps:

1. Collect and consider the most information for the decision at the time.
2. Make the decision and communicate it.
3. Move on.

Says Ransford, "As long as you do a good job and whatever you're in charge of does well, you ultimately will benefit, but not everybody sees it that way."

According to a senior executive at a small company, "The job of a leader and of managers often requires making decisions that are either not popular or have significant risk involved. Not everyone is equipped to make hard decisions. However, it is part of our responsibility as leaders and one of many reasons to be compensated at a higher level."

There also are organizations that tend to make decisions after including multiple viewpoints and interests, sometimes to extremes. "Our executive team works on a consensus model with a low risk effect," says one manager. "This makes it hard to make breakthrough decisions."

VOICES FROM THE FRONT LINES: TOUGH DECISIONS

"All tough decisions are handled immediately, whether it's following up with others or just taking care of it when obvious. Our GM is a kind man, but we have learned not to take his kindness as weakness but with respect."

"Seek recommendations on how to influence one's manager to deal more deliberately with conflict. How can one change a boss's style of conflict avoidance?"

Not all tough decisions are created equal. Depending on the human consequences and the strategic implications, different approaches are appropriate for different circumstances. The approach you take could determine whether you are viewed as firm and fair, and gain the respect of those around you. You will be either a duck or an eagle.

The Toughest Decisions

The decisions that are the toughest to make are those that affect someone else's life. Sixty percent of senior executives and managers rank hiring and firing as the toughest decisions they have had to make in their entire career.

"The toughest decisions involve life-changing experiences of the people who work with you," says one manager. Another says, "Always, the most difficult decisions are those that affect families of people that have become friends. The entire layoff process is gut-wrenching, from identifying individuals, who are friends, to performing the task."

"The HR stuff is the toughest, because it affects people," says Antonio Monteiro, chief information officer of Internet Securities, a New York–based provider of emerging-markets business information in the United States, Europe, Asia, and Latin America. "In many cases, people have put in many years with the company, and at some point you have to say, 'Your career ends here.' In some cases it is a positive because you realize you're not in a one-company career and move on. Others take it more emotionally. It's important to treat people the same way on the way in as on the way out, fairly on entry and fairly on exit."

This is part of the challenge of the transformation in company-employee loyalty discussed elsewhere in the book. In the case of Internet Securities, a highly global operation, it presents even more of a challenge because of expectations. "In ex-Soviet states and China, the expectation of what companies are expected to do is interesting, in that companies are expected to show much more loyalty to employees," says Monteiro. "But it is slowly changing."

In a layoff situation, it often is not the fault of the individuals affected but of external conditions not under an executive's or manager's control. "Over the years the toughest decision was letting someone go, not based on their performance, but based on the firm's condition," says one manager.

Another reason that dealing with others' lives is so difficult is that people represent the only sustainable competitive advantage some organizations have.

However, with bottom-line pressures, there sometimes is no choice but to make what may seem to some to be a cold, calculated decision, execute it, and move on. "We are experiencing dramatic growth, and not everybody is cut out for this kind of business, so I've had to replace wonderful and nice people with people that are sharp and skilled enough to get the job done," says an executive from the skin care industry.

The tough decisions have to be made and ultimately executed. A key in making tough decisions is to actually make them, rather than procrastinate and make a situation linger too long. Success also involves identifying the most important tough calls that need to be made and knowing when to make them.

Segment Tough Decisions by Time

Forcing the hard decisions requires that those decisions be segmented chronologically. Trying to deal with all tough decisions at the same time is pointless and, at best, can be overwhelming, resulting in deferral of all but the easiest decisions. At worst, multiple wrong decisions can be made in haste, with little regard for long-term implications. To avoid this, you should categorize tough or even significant decisions by the time frame in which they should be made.

In the case of CIO Monteiro at Internet Securities, all decisions fall into one of four time frames. Says Monteiro:

> *It's all about timing. I put decisions into four buckets: today, thirty days, a quarter, and a year. For example, a one-year decision would be to buy a new piece of infrastructure for the business. If I have a system down, that involves a decision that clearly needs to be made right away. Every decision I make falls into one of those four buckets.*
>
> *Typically, I do not rush my decisions and take as much input as possible. But to the employees, they have to know you're thinking about the decision, not deferring. You have to explain the timing to them, and you have to clearly communicate that you haven't forgotten about it.*

Decisions that are strategic generally fall into the longer time frames, while more tactical decisions end up in the shorter-term buckets. Decisions also can move between time frames. For example, if a technology vendor has licensing agreements for its software, the decision to buy moves from quarterly to daily once the purchase orders need to be signed.

Segment Tough Decisions by Level

Even if you feel that you are always the one called on to make the tough call, no one person can make all the tough decisions. Tough decisions have to be made at every level of an organization, for several reasons:

- Making the hard decisions gives ownership to the decision maker.
- More immediate ramifications of decisions can be known, the closer the decision maker is to those affected by the decision.

- With so many tough decisions required today, they cannot be centralized.
- No one has enough information to make every tough call.

Although tough decisions have to be made at all levels, it is critical that those being empowered to make the decisions have a comprehensive understanding of the vision and direction from the leadership of their organization. Otherwise, the decisions being made down in the ranks can be at odds with where the organization is headed.

At times, the decision itself is not as difficult as acting on the decision. For example, deciding to downsize staff is easier than actually telling the individuals who are being downsized. It's also difficult to redistribute the workload of those who leave to those who do not. Unfortunately, the tough call and the tough execution do not always fall to the same person, as everyone has experienced at one time or another. Says Monteiro:

I empower people to make decisions, up to a certain point. I have five lieutenants around the world, and the six of us talk about strategies. I get their input, and most of the time I go with their decisions. People will come in and say, 'My manager doesn't make decisions.' When you are tasked with the decision, it's a very different thing. I try to make sure people have the confidence to make a decision. If they make it in good faith and it ends up being a bad decision, I'm not going to jump down their throat.

In one case we had a systems engineer who rebooted a firewall, and it didn't come back. It took down the whole server. I told the manager, 'Don't let that happen again,' and it hasn't. He made a bad decision, and I pointed it out to him. He should have had a plan if it didn't work.

I'm not a big believer in democracies in business. You have to make decisions at the right level. Ninety-nine percent of people want to be led at some level. My role here is to see around corners and try to avoid issues ahead of time. I tell my managers they should be thinking a year ahead, and I'm thinking three years ahead. That's what I spend a lot of my time speaking to them about.

Tough decisions have to be made in the context of "seeing around corners," because the long-range implications of what looks like a smart decision today can turn out to be negative tomorrow. There are certain questions you should ask yourself to assure that you are considering all of the implications of those decisions.

- Who does this decision affect?
- What else does this decision affect?
- What is the long-range implication?
- Who would oppose it and why?
- What is the alternative?
- When should the decision be made?

The Five Toughest Decisions in a Career (in Order)
1. Hiring/firing
2. Changing jobs
3. Laying off others
4. Balancing work and personal life
5. Delivering bad news

Forcing Office Politics Out

Tough decisions are a consistent, everyday battle inside an organization. Sometimes, in arriving at the tough decision, you have to decide which battles you want to fight and which you can afford to save for another day, or even lose. Tough management has no place for office politics. While internal politics may be considered to be a fact of business life, it can cause great pain in making the tough calls and even dilute what should be the correct tough decision.

SURVEY: OFFICE POLITICS

When it comes to office politics in my organization, the reason(s) things are the way they are include:

Culture	74%
Types of people currently working	44%
Fostered from the top	42%
History	36%
Lack of communication	34%
Types of people hired	34%
Business pace	33%
Lack of clear direction	27%
Current economic conditions	26%
Downsizing	19%

Getting everyone to totally agree, with all interests considered, can require diluting what really should be done. This is the difference between doing the right thing and doing what everyone can agree on. At times, both can be the same, but not always. Tough management requires managers to do the right thing, which is what is best for the business and its customers.

Office politics often are ingrained in the fabric of an organization so can't easily be changed. The majority of executives and managers say that when it comes to office politics in their organizations, things are the way they are because of culture and the types of people who work there. Since neither of these is easily changed, the question is what can be done to make a situation better.

The top causes of negative office politics are personalities, gossip, and a short-term view. Another reason is that negative office politics are fostered from the top. To force the hard decisions throughout an organization, top leadership has to eliminate office politics from the tough decisions or, at the very least, minimize the influence of politics on decision making. Consider these comments from different managers:

- "Senior management fosters the negative by turning a convenient blind eye and deaf ear and by being shortsighted. The impact of their inability to deal with the office politics to the organization is low morale, slower paces of work produced, and encouraging employees not to care. Senior managers don't have the ability to deal with this escalating problem, so they ignore it."
- "The politics in our organization are clearly driven at the top. The CEO is one of the worst managers you could ever work with, but due to success during the dot-com boom, he feels that he knows more than anyone else in any field. This drives erratic and inconsistent behaviors. No priorities, no clear roles, management by getting his approval on everything. We are losing good people all the time, and I hope I am next."
- "If office politics is a problem, it's because this behavior is being rewarded, either consciously or unconsciously."

What drives negative office politics differs by company size. In large companies, ambition drives it, while in small companies, it's the personalities:

- "Office politics becomes more ingrained and more of a problem the larger the organization," says one manager at a large company. "This is because more people can succeed merely in internal terms having little to do with the customer and the outside world. Doing this well becomes their primary skill. The more complex the organization, the more this occurs."
- Says a manager at a small company: "In our small office of thirty-five people, we had two high-level managers leave, and

their replacements changed the office dynamic dramatically. Information hoarding and public humiliation of people who cross them are examples of the types of behavior that have become the norm."

- "One of the big reasons I will finish my career with a small company is the minimal role office politics play," says a senior executive at a small company.

A great downside of office politics is an increased internal focus with less focus on the customer. "People seem to go about their

---

VOICES FROM THE FRONT LINES: OFFICE POLITICS

"As the demographics of our company change, the political landscape is also changing—there is less trust in senior management now and more rumors as a result."

"The single biggest cause of negative politics is fear of change. People are looking out for themselves because they sense that no one else is. That breeds empire/domain building within the organization."

"One cannot reason a person out of a position they did not arrive at through reason. Most admin and clerical staff are emotionally based versus logical or objective. On the other hand, some totally objective people have no 'feelings' and believe everything they think before they 'think it' . . . hence, we have counterculture clashes before we get to the dreamers and the sensors! 'Twas ever thus!"

"Focus and goals at the top are clear. However, the middle management is neglected, so the message does not always reach rank-and-file employees."

---

jobs with one of two perspectives: how do I do the best job for the customer or how do I cover my rear?" says a manager at a small company.

Office politics can flourish in an organization when the behavior is rewarded, either consciously or unconsciously. "My company uses the 'good ol' boy' network," says one manager at a large company. At a small company, a senior executive says, "Human nature, including insecurities and ambition, tend to be key drivers of negative office politics. It is surprising how unaware individuals are about their own behaviors."

The reality is that some people are either working so hard or going so fast that they can miss their role in negative office politics. The best present you could buy some people is a mirror.

Top Fifteen Causes of Negative Office Politics (in Order)

1. Personalities
2. Gossip
3. Short-term view
4. Lack of caring about fellow employees
5. Ambition
6. Lack of communication
7. Grandstanding
8. Cliques
9. Rumors
10. Fostered at high levels
11. Lack of clear direction
12. Aggressive behavior
13. Taking undeserved credit
14. Thoughtlessness
15. Too much internal focus

Making the tough decision is not always easy. However, stepping up and making it proves true leadership. Many people want to follow if they have someone they believe in and who is perceived as decisive. Forcing yourself and those around you to make the tough calls and move on can make the organization run more smoothly and, most important, keep it going forward. Making tough decisions regularly also creates an environment where results become more within reach, as we discuss in the next chapter.

CHAPTER 3

FOCUS ON RESULTS

The bottom line is the bottom line. Whether a specific company focuses on profits, sales, customer satisfaction, or any other measurement, everyone in every organization faces some fundamental measurement he or she has to make, either individually, as a group member, or for a department. No matter the measure, every organization has its own type of result that matters most in various parts of that organization. While this may seem obvious to everyone, it is still easy to be distracted by the crisis of the moment throwing even the most stable manager off course.

Tough management requires that every person determine precisely what results matter most to him or her at the time and create the proper focus to achieve those results. Every action should have consequences that produce results. To focus an action on results, ask:

- How does it affect our customers?
- How does it affect our staff, employees, etc.?
- Is it on strategy?
- Who else should know about this decision?
- How does it affect the numbers?
- Is there a better action that would produce better results?

Results can be a moving target, meaning the results that matter most today may not be the ones that matter tomorrow. It is up to individuals to monitor their own result of the day, though it can be difficult to even determine what matters most when conflicting signals come from executives or managers. The key is to do more work up front, before the results are expected. Too many people end up scrambling at the last minute, seemingly incessantly, on every project or task. As a result, managers often end up working in serial fashion, since all they can do is handle the deadline of the moment. This is a losing proposition, since as tasks increase, managers hit the ceiling in terms of potential hours to work.

To keep track of what matters most at any given time takes an extraordinary amount of focus. Failure to do this properly can lead to a lack of true productivity or, at the very least, the personal sense of getting nothing done. Just because a memo from above demands some immediate action, it doesn't mean the manager should totally change gears and leave unfinished business on the table. Yes, the directive has to be dealt with, but the context of what the manager was already working on cannot be lost. Otherwise, all the time and resources spent will have been wasted, in effect making them an unrecoverable cost of business with no offsetting upside. Even though everyone is juggling more balls in business these days, it doesn't mean more can be added to the mix without negative repercussions.

For executives and managers to succeed takes more focus on the part of the individual, which is easier said than done. After the ability to communicate well, the most sought-after skill for businesspeople today is the ability to stay focused. In fact, more than three-quarters of senior executives and managers say staying focused is the most important skill for the future. (As we discussed in Chapter 1, communicating well is viewed by the overwhelming majority of managers as the number one skill necessary.)

However, with so many distractions in the business environment, retaining that focus can be difficult. With the majority of businesspeople working ten or more hours a day, and internal and external needs frequently changing, it is challenging to keep an eye on what matters most. Though you may have a great ability to focus, if superiors keep changing priorities, the focus could be wasted on what instantly becomes the wrong things.

The amount of focus determines what stays at the top of managers' lists and what gets done. However, it is very easy to end up juggling items on the list, as priorities seem to change, whether based on individual judgments or external forces. Changing priorities with the resultant shifts in focus can cause chaos in an organization.

Many top executives will say that the top priorities remain relatively constant, but this is not true at the day-to-day level of many managers. Because everything is relative to everything else, priorities naturally shift. Causes of a shift may include market conditions, required end-of-quarter results, or even personnel issues, such as a colleague calling in sick or leaving. No matter the cause, a person can end up in a different hot seat on any given day or week.

However, a larger issue of staying focused at work is the amount of information flow barraging everyone daily. Voice mail, e-mail, cell phones, instant messages, the Net, and twenty-four-hour news television can make whatever is happening at the moment look like the most important issue, causing a shift in priorities, leading to a change in focus. It is so easy today to have a crisis created by e-mail or voice mail when an executive or manager too quickly panics upon seeing a competitor's move or a change in sales.

Staying Focused at the Office

The following guidelines will help you stay focused:

- *Limit involvement.* Don't get involved in every aspect of everything going on around you. Let people do their work. In general, businesspeople will be responsible if they are truly given responsibility without second-guessing.

- *Remember strategy.* Be wary of distractions away from the over-all strategy and direction of the organization. It is important to stay focused on what matters, which should be determined in the context of the overall direction of the business.
- *Keep others focused.* It's no secret that the average attention span of some people in business can be quite short. Undoubtedly you know someone who doesn't seem to have any ability to focus other than for a few minutes, if that. This means you have to assist with that person's focus by getting to the point very quickly and clearly.
- *Pick your time.* Select the appropriate time to get something done. If you try to create a thoughtful business report in the middle of a hectic day, your report probably will not end up being that thoughtful. Individuals should identify their own best time to focus, based on the situation and tasks at hand, and then it's heads-down time.

Working Smarter

Working more hours won't cut it anymore, primarily because many managers are getting to a point where there are no more hours left to work. The only solution is to work smarter. This means translating your bottom-line, results-oriented focus all the way down to day-to-day activities and processes. This means identifying and eliminating what doesn't matter and smartly spending time on activities that will produce results.

Nowhere is working smarter more critical than in sales. With the tightening of all business, as detailed earlier, selling everything has become harder. The concept of the easy sale is only in the mind of a sales manager, as any salesperson will attest. Fewer buyers have less time to allocate to each seller, and in many cases fewer things are being bought. This leaves more sellers to compete for the time of fewer buyers. As a result, the time spent getting to a buyer and with a buyer must be well spent. No busy buyer will look kindly on anyone wasting his or her time, and the chances of the time-waster getting another audience soon after will be remote.

The Seven-Touch Approach

For salespeople, working smarter involves more planning of meetings and practice of the "seven-touch" approach to reach new buyers. The seven-touch approach means contacting the potential buyer, by various means, seven times within a four-week period. After seven touches with no success, you should set that prospect aside and move on. You can use the seven-touch approach when soliciting new business, seeking new prospects, or even keeping contact with your best customers, to make sure they stay that way. Most important, the seven-touch approach helps you to focus on results—bottom line in tough management.

Robert Flood is vice president of Westport Worldwide, an executive benefits firm of fifty employees that is a subsidiary of Hilb Rogal & Hobbs, the seventh-largest insurance brokerage in the United States, with 120 offices and about 2,500 employees. Flood's role at Westport is to market deferred-compensation plans to executives. These plans, which Westport designs and manages, provide "highly compensated" employees the ability to save beyond their 401(k)s or retirement plans. Westport clients include Marriott, Duke Energy, Liz Claiborne, Henkel Corp., and Bausch & Lomb. Flood has to appeal to the finance side of an organization, often the treasurer or chief financial officer, as well as HR executives.

"The hard part is getting into a company and talking about these programs," says Flood. "I focus on results on annual goals and then work back from that. It means figuring what I need to generate in income and adding to that by bringing in new opportunities." And that's where working smarter comes in.

No longer can Flood, or anyone selling, rely on networking and previous contacts to bring in new business, especially on high-revenue sales, such as the services from Westport. "I have to work smarter in identifying opportunities," says Flood. "I budget my time and use the Net to get as much information as I can about the company. I drill down, reviewing 10Ks and their corporate picture to help qualify my prospects. Ten years ago the information wasn't as accessible as it is today. I can do it by myself today, and technology is a big part of it. But it's like having a baby; these sales can take nine months or more."

Flood also uses the seven-touch approach, incorporating letters, voice mail, e-mail, phone calls, notes, and instant messages to reach potential clients seven times within a one-month period. Flood describes how he used the seven-touch approach with a utility company:

> *I contacted the assistant of the CFO. I called her, got her e-mail address, sent her an e-mail, sent the CFO a letter, left two voice mails, and also followed with another phone call to the assistant and set up a very good meeting. I'm careful not to be rude; that's why it's done over a period of a month.*
>
> *Before, I would give up after a few tries. Studies have shown that seven contacts are really needed because of schedules and priorities. It keeps the activity clean, and it's easy to monitor. If there is no success after the seven touches, it goes to sort of a semidead file.*
>
> *The seven touches are just to get a meeting, but we all pretty much subscribe to it. It does make me crazy sometimes, though. I'm calling on a sophisticated buyer and building a rapport with assistants. I can't come across as overbearing, or I'm dead. It keeps me up at night. The concern is that the business will not close or there are not enough good prospects in the works. The seven touches work for new prospects.*

Working Smarter and Harder

Just because you're working smarter doesn't mean that hard work is not involved. However, by combining working smarter with working harder, you can more predictably achieve better results with time left over. The key is to work smart and hard all the time that you are working, with total focus on doing only those things that pertain to the desired result. People tend to equate working more hours with working harder, which is not necessarily the case. When you are working more hours, hourly efficiency tends to decrease, and it becomes easier to lose sight of activities that best produce the desired results.

"It's so easy to let yourself get distracted," says Phil Merdinger, a principal and worldwide partner in business development at Mercer, an operational and strategic human resource consulting firm. Merdinger's role is to focus on client development, essentially finding ways to bring new business into the firm.

"Over the past several years, it's been more difficult to balance the focus on results with reality," says Merdinger. "You focus on what looked like reasonable results but then ended up being not realistic. This increases the level of frustration and anxiety. Nobody anticipated what happened to the economy. We're working harder with less resources, so we're trying to do more with less. Combine that with the fact that when the economy slows down, you start to watch the bank account. That causes you to think carefully about how to maximize your ROI on revenue generation. I have to keep my focus as narrow as possible, and you can't overinitiative yourself, taking on too many projects."

At Mercer, which has more than twelve thousand employees in about thirty countries, Merdinger finds himself focusing more on what he feels he can manage and on attaining some short-term victories by incremental actions:

As we become more of a service economy, most people assets have legs and brains and ultimately will vote with their feet. When the economy slows down, that ability to vote with feet changes. But as the economy picks up, that ability changes. You need alignment between financial goals, people, performance, rewards, and work life. I deal with it by communicating regularly, both up and down, so there are no surprises with where things stand. People end up giving me ideas for course correction.

For total focus on results, it is necessary to have a very clear focus on a manageable number of things. Otherwise, you can get spread too thin, ending up with longer and less-productive hours worked. As in the case of Robert Flood at Westport, the buying cycle Merdinger works with can be lengthy, with the risk of wasted resources if he fails to work smarter and harder.

"The challenge is that the buying cycle is stretched out more," says Merdinger. "The marketplace is much more competitive than it has been, so the cost of sales can go up, chasing things that have a marginal chance of coming through."

As a result, as can be seen in the habits of Flood and Merdinger, managers today have to put in more time up front to deliver results later. "So much information is available today, you have to do your homework," says Merdinger. "You have to understand the industry and the issues they are trying to address and relate to problems they are dealing with. You need to have your elevator speech down. You can't waste somebody's time, because you don't get that second chance."

Quick Tips for Working Smarter and Harder
- Manage expectations all the way along the line.
- Determine what, precisely, others are expecting.
- Clearly articulate your expectations of results, and solicit clear definitions of others' expectations of results.
- Communicate, clearly and frequently, the status of work toward those results.
- Quantify; put a number on everything, so progress against it can be measured.

When market conditions are tight and managers are pressed to make the numbers, the concept of working smarter and harder can

easily be forgotten. This can result not only in lost focus on ultimate goals, but also misdirection to areas that are detrimental. "It's
getting more difficult to close deals," says Merdinger, "and it
becomes tempting to eat 'road kill.' You can get the wrong customers that don't match your objectives, and it can result in bad
business. Unprofitable revenue growth, at some point, hurts. This
gets back to communicating and managing expectations of results."

Focusing on results is not necessarily something that is needed
just for a few minutes or hours, but rather something that has to
be practiced throughout the day and week. Tough management
requires a rigorous focus on what matters.

Being Productive

Who doesn't want to be more productive at work? After all, a feeling of achievement and personal accomplishment at the end of a
day or a week can be exhilarating, if not totally satisfying. However, many days seem as if they'll never end and nothing is getting
done. So why is everyone not more productive, and what would it
take to change that? The majority of executives and managers say
that to improve productivity, there should be more communication, focus, and collaboration. There also should be less office politics, meetings, and panic.

To Increase Productivity, What Organizations Need More Of
(in Order)
1. Communication
2. Focus
3. Collaboration
4. Teamwork
5. Time
6. Understanding
7. Budget

8. Direction
9. Resources
10. Technology

To Increase Productivity, What Organizations Need Less Of
(in Order)
1. Office politics
2. Meetings
3. Panic
4. Internal interaction
5. Autonomy

VOICES FROM THE FRONT LINES: PRODUCTIVITY

"The biggest productivity drains are panic fire drills for products/situations that never actually emerge, duplication of assignments to multiple people, and turf-protection restrictions on going directly to the person with the answer."

"One of the greatest inhibitors of true productivity is the sacred-cow or emperor's-new-clothes syndrome. Both cause tremendous expense of energy in areas of little opportunity and can create frustration among the working level of the organization."

"Elements that should also be included to increase productivity are customer focus, process improvement, and professional development."

"Absence of clear direction and real delegation combine with too much communication to frustrate productivity. E-mail is, in general, used very badly. 'Think before you type,' file as a draft, reread two hours (or a day) later, edit, and then think twice about whether you really need to send this! Badly used e-mail generates confusion and work, unclear delegation, and sometimes attempts at too much control."

"There is definitely too much politics and not working together to achieve the common vision. There seems to be many groups trying to justify their roles, and they drive unnecessary work, confusion, and turf wars."

"More honesty and integrity, more willingness to admit one's mistakes and to accept others' mistakes, more importance on doing it right the first time, and less importance on meeting artificial deadlines."

"Our organization's biggest problem is our 'product silos.' Each initiative on our annual business plan tends to be very department-focused—i.e., sales has its own projects, as does marketing, IT, and every other function. However, I do expect us to get better this year, thanks to a better strategic planning process that forced us to revisit and restate our mission, values, and vision. As a result, we're now focusing on just three (rather than a dozen) strategic themes that require better collaboration."

"The desire for perfection and the analysis paralysis it creates reduce productivity. Blame-proofing the responsible team is also a negative factor. Finally, the lack of clear accountability for and measurement of the results is the primary reason for lower-than-desired productivity."

"It is difficult to function as a team when everyone is pitted against each other for personal gain. Until the ability to work together is rewarded in this organization, ambition will trump effectiveness."

Delegating

Using tough management to gain results sometimes requires letting go and empowering others to execute more. As described in Chapter 1, communicating well is a key, because when subordinates understand precisely what their superior is looking for, it is much easier to be on target in delivering those results. This is also true when delegating. It is critical that those being delegated to have a deep understanding of what they are being tasked to do and know and gain access to the resources that will be needed and made available for success.

Delegation can be improved, although top executives feel that they delegate quite well, and their subordinates generally agree. The overwhelming majority (96 percent) of senior executives say

---

SURVEY: DELEGATION

In general, how well does your supervisor delegate to you, in relation to enabling you to execute against your organization's strategy and direction?

Very well	54%
Somewhat well	30%
Not very well	9%
Not at all well	3%

In general, how well do you delegate to your subordinates, in relation to enabling them to execute against your part of your organization's strategy and direction?

Very well	50%
Somewhat well	47%
Not very well	3%
Not at all well	0%

VOICES FROM THE FRONT LINES: DELEGATION

"Delegation is key in today's fast-paced environment. However, clear communication and well-understood strategies are key to the delegated manager carrying out his/her role."

"As a company, we have a mission. It ends there. Little is done to communicate what specifically our region's areas, and office's part is in that mission. In frustration our past office leader stepped aside and will ultimately leave, and I am soon to follow. I get the strong impression from our new office leader that he is having the same problem."

"If you do not delegate well in the IT services business, you are toast."

"I have learned to delegate from my employees sharing with me what I do not do well. I encourage them to ask me questions if they do not understand the assignments, my assumptions, or how the project or task ties to the big picture. We have arrived at the current positive state by working together on this issue."

"It may sound obvious, but a supervisor can only delegate well if he/she has competent (not just trained) people working for him/her. It's critical to hire well."

---

they delegate either very or somewhat well, and a large percentage of managers agree that those above them do, in fact, delegate well. However, when it comes to delegating very well, slightly over half of senior executives say they are in that category, and only 42 percent of managers say they are.

Executives and managers in larger companies report being delegated to better than those in smaller companies. In organizations with a thousand or more employees, 61 percent of executives and managers say they are delegated to very well. In organizations with fewer than a thousand employees, less than half feel they are delegated to very well.

One of the greatest challenges to delegating arises when there are fewer people to delegate to. "Over the past two years, with multiple reorganizations and inheriting mediocre performers, it has been difficult to delegate as much as I have in the past," says one manager. "I know I should be delegating more at my level, but I am also under the constraints of hiring freezes, tight deadlines, and limited skills and experience. I do more as an individual contributor, which gets the immediate work done but does not position me as an effective manager when it comes to delegation."

According to a manager at a large company, "As we have downsized, even executives are expected to be executing along with managing. Unfortunately, this has caused many to stop delegating and own the execution themselves."

At times, there also is conflict because of time constraints. "Delegation is perhaps one of the most difficult things a manager or supervisor can do," says a manager at a small company. "Many believe they can do it better and faster with fewer mistakes by handling it themselves. But it becomes a vicious circle of too much work coupled with not enough time. So do I delegate and risk errors and time crunches and getting upset, or do I do it myself and become more stressed out?"

The extent of delegation in an organization also can depend on specific supervisors and expectations. There is a difference between delegating and dumping on, and increased empowerment indicates that delegation is genuine.

"If your boss is a poor delegator, you will become one, too, in fear of carrying the label of a slougher," says one manager at a medium-sized company. Another observes, "My immediate superior has difficulties in delegating because the vice president above is not good at delegating either."

Delegating also can be a two-way street, with the supervisor not necessarily realizing that he or she can and should delegate more. "Given today's pace of life and volume of responsibilities and related activities, those who cannot delegate will perish," says one senior executive at a small company. "On the flip side, those who are unable to help their supervisor determine if what they delegate is meaningful (i.e., is a priority) will become buried and ineffective. Delegation is a matter of priority setting on both ends."

Delegation requires crystal clear communication so that people know precisely what is expected of them.

Ways to Improve Delegating
- Surround yourself with good people.
- Clearly articulate the strategy and direction.
- Make sure people understand that message.
- Check to make sure they have the proper tools and information to execute.
- Let them do their jobs.

Tough management requires letting go at all levels of management. When given the opportunity, managers generally will rise to the challenge.

Cut the Meetings

Tough management means fewer meetings. Almost no business managers see increasing the number of meetings as a way to increase productivity in their organizations. Not only that, half of executives and managers say decreasing meetings would make working in their organizations more productive, either by quantity or quality. Only 2 percent of executives and managers say that more meetings would make working in their companies more productive. Basically, nobody wants more meetings.

Part of the problem with meetings stems from what some think a meeting can accomplish. For example, good communication is the top skill for executives to succeed today. However, executives often fall into the trap of thinking that conducting a meeting where there is obvious sharing of information supplants the need for other communication. "One of my biggest challenges is convincing staff that meeting does not equal communication," says a senior executive at a small company. "Clear documentation and good prioritization foster productive communication as much as any meeting does."

However, sometimes meetings can be helpful for identifying roles and responsibilities, getting an organization more in sync. "People in my company know what to do and are given the freedom and authority to get it done," says a senior executive at a large company. "While I would prefer fewer meetings, I believe we have far fewer than other organizations our size."

An organization and its culture also help determine what role meetings play. Some meetings can be used for a leader or department head to lay out overall directions and expectations. "In our small company, it is essential that our employees have a clear understanding and direction as to policies of the company in order to handle any crisis or problem when I am unavailable," says a manager in a small company. "In order to make sure that happens, there needs to be plenty of communications and collaboration with the staff so that they have that understanding and direction." That understanding often is relayed in a meeting.

Unfortunately, other meetings are used to focus on issues that are shorter-term, which often deal with saving money rather than making it. "Productivity would improve with less internal focus and more external focus," says a senior executive at a large company. "Too many companies are focusing a disproportionate amount of their energy on short-term expense management issues, to the detriment of looking externally and focusing on growing revenue. Revenue growth efforts can energize people and improve productivity. Expense control and internal micromanagement are demoralizing."

Businesses can fall into the trap of meeting excessively to create more focus on savings, expenses, and cutting. More significantly, this focus takes eyes away from external opportunities, in the form of customers and their needs. "If people concentrated more on doing a good job for the customer and less time trying to further themselves in corporate America, the work environment would be completely different," says a manager at a medium-sized company. "Most of them don't realize that the first will result in the latter if they are truly sincere about doing a good job."

So, the next time you're running off to yet another meeting, you should stop and check whether you should even be going to it. If you are the one who called the meeting, you might want to check whether attendees also self-evaluated whether the meeting is right for them. Try answering the following questions, as well as have others attending answer them:

Is This Meeting for Me?

- Is this meeting necessary for me to attend?
- What is the potential ultimate benefit of this meeting to our customers?
- Should this meeting be canceled or eliminated for good?
- Why do we have this meeting?
- Is there frequently positive action from this kind of meeting?
- If you called this meeting, did the attendees honestly answer these same questions?

Extended Focus

Tough management also can mean looking for results in areas outside those that might consume most of a person's work life. That's the experience of Robin Ellerthorpe, a principal and director of consultants at OWP/P, a Chicago-based fully integrated architecture firm: "We find that clients are so focused on increasing the value of what they have, they're totally caught up in those results." This focus on results in a particular business or industry can cause great results in that area but leave untapped potential results from other areas not of high focus.

For example, a hospital typically spends most (if not all) of its focus on providing health care. Decisions to purchase medical devices, such as a new MRI machine, are straightforward, since the benefit and financial payback to health care professionals are intuitive. However, looking at areas outside of health care, it is not as obvious. "When they look at their facilities, they anguish because they can't see the benefit of accounting for space," says Ellerthorpe.

Like many hospitals, Lake Forest Hospital rents outside office space to medical professionals. By broadening its focus outside its traditional area of health care, the hospital discovered that it was only charging for the usable office space because that was what the tenants were technically occupying. Ellerthorpe's analysis showed that the tenants all were paying below-market rates. Once this was shown to the tenants and the hospital, the hospital increased the rents, netting an additional $750,000 per year.

Another of OWP/P's clients in the area of asset management, the State of Illinois has sixty million square feet of space. By developing and instituting processes and process improvements, including review of the leases, facility uses, and number of people working in the offices, OWP/P identified $40 million worth of savings on the state's budget of $430 million. "Processes have to show results," says Ellerthorpe.

Ellerthorpe deploys assessment teams to quantify everything. For one client, the group oversaw management of eight thousand service contracts having to do with services such as snow removal and janitorial services. Computer applications were used to catalog all the data, which then easily highlighted inefficiencies. For example, one janitor received $12 per hour, and another in the same region was being paid $30 per hour. The team then assessed all the deferred-maintenance deficiencies.

"Managers in corporations are finally beginning to realize the real estate asset," says Ellerthorpe. "It's the last frontier. Industries are so focused on their own thing, they can't see the benefit of accounting for space."

In its own organization, OWP/P also found that even though its main focus is on results from its clients, it also had to keep looking at what it does internally. The company ultimately determined that it would be more efficient to outsource the competitive tasks, such as printing and computer code writing. "Once you hit volume, it was worth it. We have to keep looking at the things we do because the markets change so quickly," explains Ellerthorpe.

Says Ellerthorpe, "I've never worked harder in my life. It's crazy hard. One of the things I used to be able to do was task things based on my e-mail. I haven't been able to file an e-mail in a folder in seven months. Everything is running in light speed now. We're in a 'now' environment, so I've had to increase my effectiveness."

Ellerthorpe also found that tough management requires a constant sharing of information, as we discussed earlier. "We're sharing all data in the consulting group. There's more common knowledge now. Everyone understands the contractual obligations."

The information flow also allows all the stakeholders to understand what is important to the organization as well as to the individual. This further allows an understanding of each person's focus and what results each person is seeking.

Be Realistic About Results

Tough management requires business leaders to be more realistic in the results they demand from those who work for them. It's no secret that many organizations have become more results oriented in recent years. The economy, market conditions, increased competition, price pressures, globalization, and more selective customers all have forced businesses to watch the bottom line more closely. Everyone is doing more with less, while even more is being expected by unforgiving shareholders and top management.

As a result, the overwhelming majority of senior executives and managers see the top management at their organizations as either extremely or somewhat demanding. And the larger the company, the more demanding is top management.

In today's business climate, it is only rational for the top brass to be highly demanding of results. "As a publicly traded company, it is all about results," says one executive. "While we can't ignore the future, we have to focus on today, tomorrow, and this quarter in order to get to the future. Our shareholders and Wall Street demand this approach, and our executive team replies responsibly."

Leaders must demand results. But that's not the issue. Top management is not always realistic about the level of results demanded and how well those results can be delivered by those below. In fact, almost 80 percent of executives and managers do not consider the results expected to be extremely realistic for them to deliver. In companies with more than ten thousand employees, almost 90 percent feel this way. Top executives have a right to place heavy demands on those who are paid to deliver results, as they are. The problem comes in setting proper expectations, based on the real capability of delivering.

"My team and I have a ton of pressure daily, weekly, monthly, and quarterly to hit our numbers," says one manager. "At times, the requests from above are not manageable or attainable, so I reset expectations on what I need (people, money, both) to run the business. I do not take higher expectations on without getting what I need to get that new job done."

Survey: **Delivering Results**

When it comes to requiring results, top management at my organization generally is:

Extremely demanding	40%
Somewhat demanding	50%
Not very demanding	10%
Not at all demanding	0%

In general, the results my superiors expect me to deliver on these days are:

Extremely realistic	22%
Somewhat realistic	62%
Not very realistic	14%
Not at all realistic	3%

When it comes to requiring results, top management at my organization generally is:

	Senior Executives	Managers
Extremely demanding	43%	37%
Somewhat demanding	50%	50%
Not very demanding	7%	12%
Not at all demanding	0%	0%

In general, the results my superiors expect me to deliver on these days are:

	Senior Executives	Managers
Extremely realistic	26%	18%
Somewhat realistic	60%	64%
Not very realistic	13%	14%
Not at all realistic	1%	5%

"I found the link to performance ratings and results is missing in my company. People do not get rated on results but how well they work with other managers. Most managers do not receive objectives, so obtaining results becomes difficult."

"Expectations far exceed reality, and no one wants to listen. Of good, fast, and cheap, the last two take priority, and the criticisms begin when it doesn't turn out well."

"The underlying theme today is metrics; if you can't measure it, you're not considering how a property is affecting your business. If you can't explain how your decisions/actions/projects are affecting the business (both positive and negative), then you aren't being an effective manager."

"Championing and rewarding results comes naturally in our organization. What we lack is bringing accountability and consequence to those not delivering results."

"In our organization the requirement, from my perspective as CEO, is to get more demanding and to put in place the capability to do that by providing feedback to managers on what is expected and how they need to drive the agenda. Real cultural change."

"IT projects and activities are hard to define in bottom-line terms on a monthly or quarterly basis, which frustrates management, who feel that they are 'just spending money' with no 'money' results."

"The current climate of business seems to be movement over real motion, chaos over correctness, and ranting over rigorous thinking. I've been with three firms as a senior executive, and all three (including two that were Fortune 200) behave this way today."

Tough management requires positive answers to two questions:

1. Do the original demands remain consistent?
2. Are those who are expected to deliver properly equipped?

"The demands are somewhat fluid," says one manager. "And what start out as realistic demands, from a financial standpoint, can turn into unrealistic ones as unforeseen problems arise with the economy and our customers."

Says another, "The single reason the result expectations are unrealistic is lack of support. People have been replaced with technology to the extent that there are too many bosses and not enough workers. Ten years ago a person in my function could have a dedicated assistant and several shared support staff. Today, the assistant has been replaced by the computer. I draft, compose, proof, print, copy, mail, and file. Instead of a ten-minute task, it is a twenty-minute task."

For tough management, it is important for top executives to stay highly demanding in requiring results, while making sure that managers receive constant feedback on how to deliver those results. When more managers face what they consider to be more realistic demands, better (or at least more predictable) numbers will be delivered.

Customer Expectations

A big payoff for tough management is at the customer level. Businesses are facing higher customer expectations today, and those who are not tough inside their organizations on issues such as clear communication, forcing hard decisions, and results orientation will pay at the customer level.

The overwhelming majority of senior executives and managers say their customers' expectations are higher than in the past. The good news is that they feel they are rising to the challenge. The

Survey: Customer Expectations

My customers' expectations versus two years ago are:

Extremely higher	23%
Somewhat higher	62%
The same	13%
Somewhat lower	1%
Extremely lower	0%

In general today, my group, department, etc., meets customer expectations:

Extremely well	37%
Somewhat well	58%
Not very well	6%
Not at all well	0%

My customers' expectations versus two years ago are:

	Senior Executives	Managers
Extremely higher	30%	15%
Somewhat higher	53%	73%
The same	16%	10%
Somewhat lower	0%	2%
Extremely lower	0%	0%

In general today, my group, department, etc., meets customer expectations:

	Senior Executives	Managers
Extremely well	42%	31%
Somewhat well	53%	63%
Not very well	5%	6%
Not at all well	0%	0%

overwhelming majority say their group, department, or organization is meeting their customer expectations, with more than a third saying they are meeting them extremely well. There's also good news for smaller companies, the majority of whom say they are meeting customer expectations extremely well.

"Customer expectations have increased noticeably," says one manager. "From our perspective, these expectations focus intensely on understanding their business, their goals, and acting as a strategic partner who can anticipate problem areas and proactively provide input and counsel."

Of course, meeting and exceeding customer expectations can cause those expectations to keep rising to new levels. "Each time a customer receives service that makes a positive impression, it becomes harder to impress that customer the next time," says one manager. "This is true for the same company as well as any other company the customer deals with."

But these higher needs on the part of customers also cause businesses to step up the pace and to push down costs, which is a key result of tough management. "My customers expect increased levels of service for less than they have historically paid for those same services," says one manager.

As a company's customers are being squeezed by market conditions, the pressure is increased all along the value chain. "All my customers are doing more with less," says a manager. "This drives up demand and expectations for the services my team provides. I, too, must do more with less, so keeping up with customer expectations continues to be my biggest challenge."

The real-time world of today, with always-on access to everyone, has changed what people have come to expect. Customers see fast-paced response in one arena and come to expect it in others. "The speed of life in general has increased in the information age," says a manager. "We as individuals or consumers expect to be instantly supplied. This is probably due to nearly instant computer responses.

This is expected now in everyone's lifestyle. Business must continue to respond accordingly."

Says another manager, "Information technology has played a significant role in raising customer service expectations, particularly from an immediate-access-to-information perspective. Customers also expect to interact with empowered employees."

According to still another manager, "In an economy where pricing is not always the most important factor, items like quality, instant turnaround, and delivery are key components for customers. Customers want to be able to talk to key players 24/7."

As customers become ever more demanding, keeping pace with their demands will become all the more difficult, especially under cost constraints. This is what tough management is all about.

Focusing on results requires a new view as to what results are being delivered and from what customers. While all customers are important, not all are of the same value to a company. Segmenting customers by value potential will become more common, so the best customers will continue to get the best service. The rules of tough management will satisfy higher customer expectations, which can, in turn, provide the motivation for new ideas, approaches, and performance. Those who miss this will simply lose the business.

Recharge the Workplace

It's time for people in business to take steps to recharge the workplace. The majority of executives and managers are optimistic about the future of the economy and business growth. Managers and workers have come out of a few difficult business years with increases in workload and decreases in company loyalty. For those who made it through the tough times and effectively performed more than one job, the unending, continuous workload can be wearing.

However, since optimism finally is creeping back into the business leadership and growth is projected, this is the time to take a deep breath and get ready to go. Unlike the toiling of the past few years, with tightened budgets, decreased business, and downsizing, much of the future workload will be based on business growth. It doesn't mean there will be less work, but with increased customer activity, the work can feel less like treading water.

Recharging the workplace involves remotivating the individuals in that workplace. This means everyone from top executives and managers to the workers, many of whom are the face of the company to the customer. Individuals can take a few steps to help get charged for the work ahead:

- *Change something, whether the job or the actual work at the job.* Many businesspeople are looking for new work. This does not mean they want to change companies, but they want to do something different. Unfortunately, some executives tend to keep someone in the same job because the person is performing that job very well. This is just the opposite of what should occur if that person has been performing that job for a long time. People need change in work to keep it interesting. Doing the same thing day after day, week after week, no matter how interesting the tasks, can become less challenging and less rewarding. Take a look around the company, look for people who have been doing the same thing for a long time, and check whether they are happy.

- *Stop and think about what you do every day.* If it is repetitive (and there is no practical way to change jobs at this time), freshen your approach to the job itself. One way to do this is to reset your priorities. Basically, think about how you could approach your work differently. Perhaps there is a better way to do your job or an innovative way to approach it and make it more integrated with, say, someone else's job.

- *Take it upon yourself to learn something about your business or organization.* For example, if you're nontechnical, learn something about technology. If you're in finance, go learn something directly from customers. If you're in customer service, go learn something from finance.

People in business need to continue to learn and grow.

Those in the workforce want to be inspired and motivated by their leaders. Executives and managers say that to maintain or improve employee loyalty in the future, companies should increase or improve, among other things, advancement opportunity.

Though sometimes a bit unsettling in the beginning, change for people in business can be very healthy and, ultimately, make them more productive. Fresh, recharged executives or managers will also tend to be innovative, as they bring new energy to what someone else might have viewed as the same old job. As long as management makes it clear what is expected in the new position and how it will be measured, the new person can focus on delivering on those results. And that's what tough management is all about.

CHAPTER 4

REMAIN FLEXIBLE

The longer someone does something, the easier it is for the person to keep doing that same thing. The same is true for groups, departments, and entire organizations. Activities become routines and, ultimately, habits. Comfort sets in, and anyone doing that "something" feels challenged when someone wants to change it. While some of these habits might be positive, many are not. Tough management requires that managers identify habits, challenge and break them, and insert an added degree of flexibility into their work life.

Even while communicating effectively, forcing the hard decisions, and focusing on results, individuals must organize themselves to remain flexible enough to change directions quickly when necessary and adapt to changing conditions. The ability to recognize and adapt to change is ranked at the top of the list of important leadership qualities for executives and managers. Being flexible can help decrease the mounting stress levels on those managers.

Flexibility is critical for the manager today because it is the relief valve in a world of work where executives and managers continually face increased stress, an increased volume of work, and mounting numbers of projects. Without a good dose of flexibility, you can end up in a situation where work controls you rather than the other way around.

The Spiral of Stress at Work

The stress level of executives and managers is not going down. Eighty-two percent of senior executives and managers are stressed at work, with more than a fourth feeling highly stressed. Interestingly, one-fourth of managers feel they are more stressed than their bosses, one-fourth feel their bosses are more stressed than they are, with the remaining half saying they and their superiors are equally stressed.

While some stress at work can be positive, giving businesspeople a heightened awareness and a slight edge, high stress is not conducive to good decision making. Decisions can be rushed, arrived at with little thought, and in essence, just made to be expedient. Tough management requires that stress levels be decreased, which is possible, or that tough decisions be made while not at the height of working on unrelated activities.

The top stress causes are deadlines, customer demands, and conflicting responsibilities. And therein lies the problem. Deadlines drive managers to shorter vantage points, as they focus on delivering in the here and now. The intense attention to deadlines, which obviously increases personal pressure, takes away any potential for flexibility. Many managers are working from deadline to deadline, with no breathing room or time for assessment. These pressures come from several sources:

- *The managers' superiors.* "Most of my stress is due to the management style of our CEO," says one manager. "He is inconsistent, lacks process, and is still trying to run things as an entrepreneur versus a CEO."
- *Peers.* "If it was just meeting customer and board expectations, there would be very little stress," says a manager. "Unfortunately, we have a very competitive manager team, and the majority of my stress comes from team member coalitions and power jockeying."

- *Subordinates.* "[For me] as a leader, manager, and supervisor, sustaining a motivated and well-aligned staff consumes more energy than necessary," says one executive. "Raising children is less stressful than managing adults who struggle with taking personal responsibility."

"Unreasonable demands from management were the primary source of stress in my life," says yet another executive. "I was working for a leader who continued to espouse an unrealistic do-even-more-with-even-less mentality. My main role was to be a buffer for the staff. Fortunately, I switched to a different position with a more focused set of responsibilities and more realistic expectations. Life is too short to continue in a situation in which the ordinary stresses are added to by an unreasonable management."

"The most stress comes from executives in IT," says an information technology manager. "They are contradicting one another and are prone to changing decisions after they have been communicated. They might have reached their level of incompetence."

SURVEY: STRESS AT WORK

When it comes to my stress level at work, I feel:

Highly stressed	26%
Moderately stressed	55%
Slightly stressed	17%
Not at all stressed	2%

My stress situation can best be described as:

I am more stressed than my superior.	26%
My superior is more stressed than I am.	27%
My superior and I are equally stressed.	41%
None of us is stressed.	2%

"Incompetence of superiors when setting deadlines is an issue," says another.

"I have been in this business for over thirty years, and the stress levels just keep climbing, making the CEO position less and less desirable," says the head of a small company. "It used to be fun to make things happen and meet goals and objectives for our company, but now it is becoming a chore, with few rewards other than money, and even that can't compensate for the stress."

VOICES FROM THE FRONT LINES: STRESS AT WORK

"Significant amount of work with less staff to delegate. This creates a situation where my best assets are not being used, as the daily activity is keeping me from more focused time on business growth and new revenue streams."

"If it weren't for stresses, work would be fun."

"Changing business models introduce uncertainty and learning new ways of working—which is great but adds stress."

"The pressures in any medium to large corporation are very high and only going to get worse due to increased measurement and thus management of performance data. The expectations in and speed of business in the past two decades have increased massively. Corporations may need to offer on-site counseling all the time."

"We are a professional firm, and in our case, it is a matter of staffing. Finding qualified, willing staff has been a struggle at both the management and professional level."

"Uncertainty due to merger issues has paralyzed head count, projects, and product development."

Says another manager, "The biggest stress is dealing with people issues. Keeping everyone focused on the same outcome even though each of them has different responsibilities and therefore a different perspective is the biggest challenge."

As everyone at work struggles to do more with less, some are ending up with tasks that used to be handled by others, adding to the stress.

Top Ten Causes of Stress at Work (in Order)
1. Deadlines
2. Customer demands
3. Conflicting responsibilities
4. Budget constraints
5. Number of hours worked
6. E-mail overload
7. Lack of downtime
8. Pressure from above
9. Meetings
10. Expectations of others

So Much to Do, So Little Time

Managers cannot be rigid because they simply have too much to do in the course of a day, week, or month. Over the years, executives and managers have evolved into working longer and longer days.

The volume of tasks that managers face daily can be daunting. For example, if you keep a list of things to do during the workday, you are like the overwhelming majority of businesspeople. And if you don't complete all the tasks on your list, you're just like everybody else. The majority of lists contain six to ten items, while one-third of businesspeople keep lists of eleven to twenty items. The good news is that those lists have a purpose, ranging from keeping managers on track to setting priorities.

SURVEY: DAILY LISTS

How long is your list of things to do during the workday?

1–5 items	8%
6–10 items	38%
11–20 items	32%
21–40 items	11%
More than 40 items	6%
I keep more than one list.	9%
I don't keep a list.	5%

If you keep a list of things to do during the workday, generally what percent of your list is completed daily?

0%	1%
1%–10%	6%
11%–30%	21%
31%–50%	21%
51%–70%	27%
71%–99%	19%
100%	1%

"A list helps me keep focus and directs me to complete daily goals and objectives," says a manager at a small company. "Keeping a list provides me with a useful record of progress toward goals," says one at a large company. "The decision about whether an item makes it onto my list is important, because the simple act of adding an item to the list makes it clear that it is worth spending time on."

These lists are not static, with some changing on a recurring basis, pointing to the need for increased flexibility. "My list is constantly evolving, and the projects on it always span over time periods that exceed a day," says a senior executive at a small company.

According to a manager at a larger company, "My to-do list is built fresh every morning as the first item I do each day. I prioritize the list based on due date, effort required, and criticality. I assign my time so that I ensure larger tasks get worked on every day and I don't get caught up in all the little stuff."

Executives and managers have several reasons for keeping lists:

- *Predetermining the day.* Lists help determine just how much you have to do in a given day, so they help you determine when that workday might end.
- *Keeping track.* People cannot handle and remember too many topics at any one time, so lists do that for them.
- *Insurance.* If it's on the list, it's not likely to be forgotten, even if not dealt with at a given time.

Though lists are essential for most, tough management requires that managers not get obsessive about those lists. Too much emphasis on the list can improve tactical effectiveness but cause a manager to lose flexibility for dealing with unforeseen issues that may, in fact, be more strategic in terms of the organization's goals than what is being addressed on the list at any given moment. To remain flexible, managers have to vary from using lists on occasion and constantly recalibrate what truly matters. Managers then keep synchronizing their lists with what matters most at the moment, in line with long-term objectives.

Rules for Effective Lists
- Keep it short. When too many items are on a list, many tasks wind up near the bottom, with little chance of ever getting accomplished.
- Sort lists into two: one for short-term tactics and the other for more significant objectives. The latter should be short.
- Keep it focused.

- Pick your productive list time. The only way to shorten some lists may be to come in early or stay late occasionally.
- Be realistic. Before you list a task, be sure it is doable.
- Review it. Make sure items on the list still should be there.

VOICES FROM THE FRONT LINES: DAILY LISTS

"Lists tend to become obsolete so quickly that they're almost not worth making up. Some days I try to focus on the top third of what I need to do to assure I give the most important work the most attention."

"I could make the list as long as I want, since there are countless things that I could do if I choose to. If the list is more than ten items long, I'm not doing a good job of prioritizing and/or delegating, and tracking the size of my list is a good gut check of my management effectiveness."

"I'm trying to wean myself from paper lists and use the list in my PDA. So far, I have not been successful because I like to see everything I need to do in one place and I'm continually prioritizing and reprioritizing based on the changing environment."

"Sometimes I come in with a long list and get none of the items accomplished. Other times I come in and blow through my list quickly enough to get other things taken care of. The latter [scenario] is much rarer."

"I generally start by completing an easy item before trying to tackle the top-priority item."

"The only list that I keep is for long-term, strategic projects for which I need to be preparing and prioritizing."

"Too much to do, too little time, lack of staff, lack of appreciation, therefore easy to lose focus."

"I keep a running list in categories but highlight the things I really, really want to get done today."

"The number of incoming items and areas requiring vigilant monitoring continues to replace if not outpace the speed at which items can be considered complete."

Push Back

When Lou Gerstner first took over IBM, he encountered internal "pushback," which involved traditional, longtime IBMers essentially telling Gerstner why something he wanted to do would not work. Pushback comprised not so much acts of defiance, but more of an attitude of "Look, we've been here a long time, and we know what works and what doesn't, and what you are proposing will not work." The reality was that Gerstner was attempting not the incremental moves that had been tried before, but steps that would lead to total culture and business transformation inside the company. That pushback era was at the height of the buildup and ride through the Internet boom time, when Gerstner wanted to transform the company into a pervasive e-business enabler, which he ultimately did, despite the pushback.

We are now in a new time where pushing back is required for you to stay flexible enough to get done what you must and still have any sense of sanity around the office. With everyone required to do more with less, tough management calls for serious pushing back and getting others to rethink what they are demanding of you. The reason is the change in the business climate today, with work increasing but staffing lagging behind.

"Part of it has to do with the market coming back," says Janet Smalley, senior director of brand research and business intelligence at Marriott International. "It's beginning to look hopeful, so people are starting to think about the future again."

Smalley leads the research efforts for Marriott and Renaissance hotel brands and, like many managers, finds herself with more to do than there is time to do it. Though Marriott has institutionalized the ten-hour workday, Smalley often finds herself working ten to twelve hours daily just to get what is required done. She explains the challenge this way:

> *In the lodging industry, things are happening faster than they used to. Brands are getting a lot more competitive and savvy about marketing and PR. When I worked at Marriott back in the late eighties and early nineties, it used to be a polite industry. It's much more competitive, and we have to change quickly now, and there are a lot more brands, and the consumer has changed.*
>
> *Ten years ago, the business traveler just wanted a bed and to get in and out. The consumer has gotten a lot more demanding, and travel is a lot more difficult since September 11 [2001]. The expectations have gone up. Part of it is because people have put a lot more money into their homes during that time, so they are used to higher expectations for conditions.*

Like many managers, Smalley finds herself fielding an increasing number of requests from her customers—in this case, other Marriott divisions and executives, all of whom are trying to satisfy increasing demands from *their* customers. Says Smalley:

> *I've gotten a lot better at saying no. I found that since September 11 changed everything in how we do business, so we're saying sort of yes to a request, but not the way you asked it. People are pretty reasonable.*
>
> *For example, we've been looking at guest room technology and looking at better televisions, flat panels, LCDs for guests to con-*

nect from laptops, iPods, whatever. The person in charge came to me to test the assumption that guests would pay for that connectivity. I spent ten minutes with him and let him talk, and the more he talked, the more he realized he could convince the leadership that guests would not, at this time, pay—the market for that connectivity just wasn't large enough yet. It made no sense to do a study to find out.

I find it's worth the investment of having a live discussion, and I find myself encouraging conversations. Not more meetings, just more conversations.

I'm probably more productive today because now I just push back more, focusing on the things that are most important. I have the ability to say I'm focused on this right now but have flexibility in that I don't shut my door.

This is a key to tough management: make sure that you are focused on the most important issues at the moment, but stand ready to change gears, even if only momentarily, when the situation truly warrants it. Each "interruption" has to be weighed in context of your top goals as well as its relevance to what you are working on at the moment. This also will help reduce the level of stress.

Morphing to Be Flexible

One way to remain flexible is through morphing, where you essentially take the shape of the environment. This doesn't mean changing who you are, but rather totally adapting how you act and what you do based on the current work environment in which you are living at the moment.

For example, two-hundred-year-old DuPont, the oldest industrial company in the Fortune 500, found itself in the midst of a major shift in the late 1990s, as the knowledge economy took hold in the marketplace. DuPont had been essentially an explosives company during the 1800s and a chemicals, energy, and materials company in the 1900s, launching such notable brands as Teflon, nylon, Lycra, Stainmaster, and Kevlar. To prepare for the next century, DuPont reorganized itself around the concept of "One DuPont" with the focus of creating science-based solutions for customers. The refocus on customers was similar to the approach Gerstner took when he stepped in at the helm of IBM.

DuPont, with almost sixty thousand employees, created a new mission: to achieve sustainable growth and increase shareholder value through integrated science- and knowledge-intensive products and businesses. An additional component was added to the mission statement as well: to achieve sustainable growth and increase shareholder value through productivity gains using Six Sigma (a quality improvement process for achieving close to zero defects). The objective was to take 15 to 25 percent of DuPont's annual revenue out of its annual cost base, translating, in effect, to cost savings in an amount equal to up to a quarter of the company's revenue.

The Six Sigma concept of measuring defects was created in the 1980s to apply a universal quality metric regardless of product complexity. Companies such as General Electric, Motorola, and AlliedSignal proved that Six Sigma worked, and many other companies followed their example.

In general, Six Sigma had been deployed at companies to make processes more efficient by eliminating waste and its associated costs. Higher sigma values indicate better products, and lower sigma values represent less desirable products, regardless of the product. The higher the sigma level, the fewer defects there are per unit made or service delivered. In products produced at a six-sigma level of quality, only 3.4 defects are detected per million opportunities. Companies typically operate at four sigma, or 6,210 defects per million opportunities. DuPont was looking to use Six Sigma to radically cut its costs, since it is such a large producer.

After Six Sigma was well under way throughout DuPont, the company found itself morphing to remain flexible. "Six Sigma is about cost reduction and increasing productivity," says Don Linsenmann, the vice president in charge of the Six Sigma implementation at DuPont. "We brought in a very special tool kit that dealt with cost reduction and got quite good at that. We became master craftsmen at cost reduction."

However, while DuPont had repositioned itself for the new century, with its new mission and literally thousands of successful Six Sigma projects going on worldwide, the markets began to change again, requiring a great amount of flexibility on the part of the company. Says Linsenmann:

> *The outside world started changing, requiring top-line growth. There were mega trends, such as globalization, emerging markets, and increased pricing of oil and natural gas. It put such pressure on change that you can't solve that dislocation only by cutting costs. We needed an engine to grow and get bigger.*
>
> *We had a set of tools that we knew worked on cost reduction. We looked at how we could apply these same tools in a new area. We started gaining confidence that the tools were working, and we began morphing them into a new space. Looking for double-digit growth using existing Six Sigma tools for top-line growth is a lower risk way to go.*

DuPont deployed tools such as process maps used to identify critical tasks, the early identification of desired outcomes, and sophisticated computer tracking systems. However, morphing to focus more on top-line growth than on cutting costs did not start companywide. Linsenmann describes the process:

> *Morphing starts locally. One group that did not have a priority to focus on costs, but rather growth, since it had plenty of capacity, was the Crop Protection Group. They said they needed to grow*

their top line. In that one location, the people were comfortable to use the tools in a new way. That node of deployment started TLG (top-line growth). It was a change management/early-adapter model. They had unused capacity to produce products in their business.

If I had said, "Let's drop Six Sigma on a cost-savings basis and jump to TLG," it wouldn't have worked. That would have been transforming, not morphing. You have to motivate, listen, and coach people into the new space.

The flexibility of how we deploy things place to place to place is predicated on learning more from others. If you're morphing because you're part of this whole organism, you can launch because you can succeed without all of the homework. Stealing shamelessly from each other reduces your workload. We're trying to put more value on the collaboration and reuse of learned practices. Transformation now is all about collaboration with your colleagues to grow the company and solve our customers' problems.

DuPont's move toward using Six Sigma for revenue growth from its initial focus on cost savings happened over a period of time and was a process, not an event. Morphing can be the best way to remain flexible, by starting relatively small and using tools, methods, or processes that you already have proved work for a different outcome.

Stop Something

Sometimes tough management requires being tough. This means being the one who calls a halt to a direction, a project, a process, or any action in the business that, for whatever reason, seems to be moving forward for the wrong reasons.

For example, many managers and employees are grossly overloaded and can't possibly finish every project or program that's been started. This leads to personal frustration and lost opportunity, due to lack of resources.

During the growth economy of the nineties, the great challenge was for companies to decide what not to do. Market valuations drove investment spending, Internet startups challenged fundamental businesses at every turn, and many organizations sought market share increases by expanding into new areas. It was the time of the great upside: so many opportunities, so little time.

As a result, companies became quite adept at turning down certain opportunities or projects. They learned how to decide what not to do. This knowledge carried through the economic downturn of recent times, with companies turning down more and more projects, as budgets tightened and downsizing ensued. Problem is, many companies did not institute processes to stop things they were doing, but focused more on scaling back the launching of new projects.

One organization that institutionalized the stopping of projects is Premier America Credit Union, one of the strongest credit unions in the United States, with more than $1.0 billion in assets and more than seventy thousand members. According to John M. Merlo, Premier America's president and CEO, "A drop list is required by departments, and it gets approved as part of the annual budget."

The credit union generally drops four or five "things" a year, such as closing a branch or dropping a product that is no longer a growth opportunity. "We've done this for seven straight years," says Merlo. "It helps to reallocate resources to focus on what matters."

In the case of DuPont, senior executives held a series of meetings to determine what should be stopped and simply stopped those projects.

Whether you adopt the annual process approach of Premier or the "event" approach of DuPont, it is essential that you proactively identify and stop appropriate projects.

VOICES FROM THE FRONT LINES:
DIFFICULTY IN STARTING/STOPPING PROJECTS

"Starting projects, processes, products, etc., is too easy, as no one wants to be perceived as getting in the way of innovation and progress. Having an effective governance process to prioritize and manage initiatives, processes, products, etc., is what separates successful from unsuccessful organizations. Stopping old initiatives, processes, products, etc., that should be replaced by the new product and process should be built into the approval process for all new initiatives."

"My experience is that once a project and a program get started, it is very difficult to stop the project/program. There is always someone in the organization that will advocate for a project's continuation. The job of stopping a project rests with senior leadership."

"Once budget is allocated and the project takes on a life of its own, it is hard to stop but has to be done, especially in tough times."

"The main problem is not the starting or stopping; it is moving a project forward in a timely way."

Starting a project is not all that difficult in an organization. In fact, fewer than 20 percent of executives and managers say it is either extremely or very difficult to start one. "To start new projects is not difficult," says one senior executive at a small company. "To sustain them is sometimes tough due to competing demands on staff and other resources." While starting a project is not difficult, it is not necessarily what many companies are looking to do.

However, when it comes to stopping a project or process in an organization, it's a different story, with almost 40 percent of top leaders saying that stopping something is extremely or very difficult. "People find it difficult to give up even if the project is not viable," says one manager.

One of the primary reasons for this is that to get a project started, people become vested. They have "skin in the game" and gain a sense of ownership of a project. "Projects take on a life of their own," says a manager at a large company. "People tend to become very protective once they get on a project." Says a senior executive at a medium-sized company, "It's harder to stop something as people have invested in the planning and selling of an idea. Once it starts, there's a lot of face-saving to be done to stop it."

The reality is that it is awkward, at best, for the person who pushed hard for approval or funding of a project to go back and say things are different now, so the project should be killed. But tough management requires precisely this selfless approach, for two reasons:

1. This business environment is one of the most difficult many companies have faced in years. Customer demand is down, traditional buyers have scaled back, and many companies are tentative about growth because of the uncertainty of the future.
2. Companies are shorthanded; workers who were not downsized out of a job are forced to absorb increasing workload from those who were. "We're so shorthanded these days, due to budget cuts, that everyone already has too much on their plates," says one manager.

This means getting past the concept of deciding what not to do and taking a proactive stance to stop doing something. Stop a project, a meeting, or even a product line that most employees realize is dead (even if not buried!).

With slow- or no-growth budgets, increasing market pressures, and lack of corporate appetite for new investments, there's not a lot of room to start new projects in an organization. Though stopping projects might sound like retrenchment, it actually is a method of stimulating business growth. By quickly stopping a project that might be doomed to a dead end anyway, you create a void to fill with something that is worthwhile today, with more realistic returns.

E-Mail: The Flexibility Killer

As if all the deadlines causing stress and the heavy workload weren't enough to make you keep your head down, there is the dreaded volume and velocity of e-mail to help fill out the day. E-mail can become so consuming that it can take away any sense of flexibility, especially when it causes you to get lost in the messages of the moment, taking you away from what should be the important focus for the long term.

It is difficult to be flexible when a day is filled with the crisis of the moment, the laundry list of things to do, phone calls, person-

---

SURVEY: E-MAIL MANAGEMENT

How much time daily do you spend sending, receiving, reading, and writing e-mail?

Less than 15 minutes	1%
15–30 minutes	5%
31–60 minutes	19%
1–2 hours	45%
3–4 hours	23%
More than 4 hours	7%

How much of the e-mail you receive do you personally deem "unnecessary"?

76%–100%	8%
51%–75%	33%
26%–50%	43%
0%–25%	17%

VOICES FROM THE FRONT LINES:
E-MAIL MANAGEMENT

"While there is definitely too much e-mail, I learn something new every day from an e-zine article or white paper that appeared in my mail. I try to at least scan before deleting."

"E-mail is an excellent communication tool. It is unfortunate that there are so many individuals that abuse it and misuse it. It gets a bad rap, and it shouldn't!"

"Mostly, I just read what I think is important and ignore the rest. Sometimes I miss things, but someone usually follows up on the really, really important items."

"The increase in e-mail is largely due to spam. It is becoming intolerable. Our business depends on receiving many e-mail inquires regarding our product from previously unknown individuals, so it is not possible to use typical antispam software to filter the junk e-mail. Legislation may not be the cure-all, but it would certainly help to reduce this unwanted and time-consuming distraction."

"Some of the e-mail overload is of my own choice. The Internet, with its discussion forum capacity, is a good way to interact with other professionals on complex subjects and stay current. So I view some of the load as being part of a virtual watercooler effect."

"The problem is that while people are taught to use the software, they are not taught how and when to use e-mail itself. Companies need to have an e-mail strategy that needs to be rigidly enforced from the top downward. There has never been a better method for people to pass the monkey on to someone else."

"The bulk of the two hundred to three hundred e-mails I receive daily is expected and automatically sorted into folders that I search if I have a question in a particular content area. These are then stored in searchable archives every few months. Otherwise, I just deal with the five to twelve exceptions and personal mail that come through the screening."

"E-mail overload is a corporatewide issue. We use e-mail to replace phone calls, memos, face-to-face discussions, and advertisements, leaving individuals to sort through a (growing) daily barrage of disparate content."

"E-mail gets more of my attention than phone calls or paper communication. E-mail is very difficult to ignore and somehow demands an immediate response!"

"E-mail has become the vehicle of choice to avoid direct interaction with people. Too many people overcommunicate by passing on far too much information or feeling the need to respond to every message they receive, even the ones that are (arguably) only informational and require no action."

"Generally receive e-mails only from those that I expect activity, and review the subject before opening and reading (some deleted without reading). Receive very little junk mail or spam. One-third of e-mails considered info only, scan read and deleted with no response. One-third of e-mails require response—some quick responses and a few requiring up to ten minutes or more in response time (many with attachments)."

"I read everything, even if it kills me."

"Junk e-mail, spam, etc., is soon going to ruin this medium of communication. I am to the point that I will absolutely under no circumstances purchase a product or service from any company that sends me unwanted e-mail marketing materials. I have started to reply to some companies to that effect, as I have asked to be deleted from their broadcast e-mails."

nel issues, and then perhaps a few hours of e-mail writing and reading, all in the same day. Three-fourths of senior executives and
managers now spend an hour or more a day sending, receiving,
reading, or writing e-mail, and a third spend three or more hours
a day. By the time all this is done, any sense of flexibility is gone
until too late in the day.

E-mail overload is out of control, threatening to negate the
great productivity of fast, ubiquitous electronic communications.
The U.S. Postal Service handles about 203 billion packages in one
year. By contrast, that number of e-mail messages is sent in about
six days. By 2006, the total number of e-mails sent daily is
expected to top 60 billion, or roughly 22 trillion a year, according to researcher IDC. Of that e-mail, about 40 percent of it is
the unwanted kind (spam), according to antispam software company Brightmail. And this spam is more than a personal hassle;
it has a real cost to businesses. A company with ten thousand
employees suffers more than $13 million worth of lost produc-
tivity, says research firm Gartner. Including lost productivity,
additional equipment, software, and people hired to fight the
problem, spam is expected to cost U.S. businesses roughly $10 bil-
lion a year.

This is only part of the picture. The real hit is being felt at the
individual level, as managers and employees spend hour after hour,
day after day, scrolling through message after message, trying to
sift through to those that matter. "E-mail is killing me," says a vice
president in an $8 billion company, who gets more than a hundred
messages a day.

However, it's not just spam that is causing the overload. There
are two other abuses of e-mail: the "self-protection" copies and the
dreaded "reply all" messages to everyone on trivial matters.

However, on the positive side, most in business see e-mail as an
excellent communication tool, when used properly, allowing executives to communicate the same message to all simultaneously.

Neither spam nor the increase in volume of e-mail is likely to
occur soon, but managers still need a breather from e-mail over-

load. Tough management requires that managers take steps to control e-mail in order to remain flexible:

- If any subject or issue involves more than two e-mails, one party should call the other to resolve the issue by phone.
- No junk e-mail; no jokes.
- Send only relevant information—that is, what the person needs to know.
- Limit CCs (copies), which might be more appropriately named CYA.
- Don't play Ping Pong with e-mail for a conversation; use the phone.
- Deal with it and delete it.
- Don't read every e-mail as it comes in; handle messages in batches.

Top Ways Executives and Managers Deal with E-Mail Overload (in Order)
1. Delete messages without reading them
2. Read only messages from known sources
3. Use filtering software
4. Send fewer CCs
5. Use multiple accounts

The One-Week E-Mail Challenge

Pick a week, any week, maybe a summer week, and do not use any e-mail. None. Don't read any; don't write any. Do not use instant messaging (that would be cheating). Your children might think you're nuts trying to live a week without e-mail, but challenge them to try it. Not much would necessarily be missed.

A third of executives and managers rank 51 to 75 percent of their e-mail as unnecessary, and almost half of them say that up to half of the e-mail they receive is unnecessary. Almost two-thirds delete e-mails without reading them.

In just one week without e-mail, the majority of managers would pick up five to ten hours per week. The time could be used for face-to-face meetings with employees and customers; it could be used to call someone. The extra time could even be used for just thinking. Any critical issue you missed in an e-mail will be brought to your attention. You can be sure that if it's that important, you'll hear about it.

Managers need a break, and there aren't many places to find one. After your week away from e-mail, don't go back and read all of it; you'll never catch up. Just start fresh with e-mail that arrives the day you start using it again.

Company Longevity

Another aspect of remaining flexible has to do with your personal career track. Already facing earning pressures and increasingly demanding customers, executives and managers face another potentially more serious issue on the horizon: the longevity of key personnel. The amount of time executives and managers plan to stay with their organizations is changing, with the majority now planning to stay years rather than decades:

- When asked how long they expected to remain at an organization five to ten years ago, almost half say they would have planned to stay more than ten years, with nearly half of those saying they expected to stay twenty or more years.
- Today, only one-fourth of those same executives and managers say they expect to stay with the same organization for more than ten years.
- Another 16 percent place their tenure at work in the two- to three-year range, a time frame hardly considered several years ago.

SURVEY: COMPANY LONGEVITY

In the past (five to ten years ago), I would have expected to stay working for the same organization:

0–1 year	0%
2–3 years	4%
4–5 years	17%
6–10 years	31%
11–15 years	15%
16–19 years	12%
20 or more years	21%

Today, I would expect to stay working for the same organization:

0–1 year	2%
2–3 years	16%
4–5 years	23%
6–10 years	32%
11–15 years	12%
16–19 years	5%
20 or more years	10%

I feel this way because of:

Employer loyalty/lack of loyalty	48%
Leadership of organization	42%
Work-life balance	38%
Current economic conditions	38%
Organizational culture	35%
Other/better opportunities	24%
Personal financial gain	24%
Downsizing	20%
Past experience	20%

Recent experience	16%
Geographical concerns	12%
Other	12%
Family's/relatives' experiences	9%
Outsourcing	7%
Recent family freedom	5%
Tradition	4%
Post-9/11 concerns	2%

The number one reason is employer loyalty (or lack of loyalty). "The social contract between employer and employee has disappeared, thanks to actions by both parties," says one manager. "We are in a world of every company and every individual for themselves, a sad and unproductive condition." Says another, "Companies care less and less for their employees and more and more for production at any cost, which is very dangerous for the future."

The other leading reason managers plan to work at the same organization for a shorter period of time is the leadership of the organization. "Everyone extols the virtues of loyalty, honesty, commitment, but very few executives and CEOs practice the principles preached to the employees," says one manager.

In a world of mergers and consolidations, the leadership of at least part of the ultimate organization changes, with a cascading effect throughout the troops. As many in upper management experience less job satisfaction, they focus more on the bottom line, which can cause less investment in employees. "As companies change, they redefine themselves," says one manager. "Mutual commitments are only good until things change. Commitments do not extend automatically once a company changes their side of the arrangement."

When executives and managers leave, much knowledge goes with them. Relationships, both external and internal, can take great time and resources to replace, if they are replaceable. Tough management requires that this be recognized and dealt with before the exodus begins.

Living the "What If" Life

It's not enough just to be flexible in matters at work. With the changing social contract between employee and employer, managers must also remain more flexible in their personal careers. They can do this by living what I call the "what if" life at work. This means you should be constantly evaluating and reevaluating work scenarios that can affect you personally. For example, ask, "What if business drops dramatically in my area?" or "What if my boss moves to a different department?" or "What if the new CEO doesn't work out?" This is not to say you should become totally paranoid about what *might* happen. However, you should have a game plan and an approach for almost any potential occurrence that could affect you. These days, it is critical to constantly evaluate, if even momentarily, what you would do if X happened.

Gone are the days of getting out of college and working for one institution until retirement, with full pensions intact. Several factors are driving this change:

- Employers generally are looking to get each job or task done the best and most efficient way possible. Economics or skills can drive organizations to shift work away from one employee to another place, whether to a different department or location, or to total outsourcing. Though nothing personal is involved, the manager or employee takes the hit.
- Business pressures such as competition and the need for increasing financial returns relentlessly drive companies to look for

cheaper ways to do things. This can lead to reorganizations, mergers, acquisitions, spin-offs, or asset sales.

- New executives bring with them new ways to do things, which do not always involve the current people who are doing them the old way. With executives and managers changing companies more frequently, more ripple-effect changes will be felt throughout organizations.

- Many individuals do the same job for too long and become comfortable and complacent. As innovation continues in the competitive marketplace, the comfort zone causes those in it to stagnate until the business has to take drastic action, again hurting the individual.

Your Virtual Enterprise

Tough management requires being realistic in how you view your relationship with the corporate entity for which you work. This doesn't mean there should be no company loyalty, but that loyalty to yourself should be more prominent. Essentially, you should view yourself as your own virtual enterprise.

Kimberly Barnes has always been attracted to potentially high-growth companies that have a specific business problem. After an early career in sales at Xerox, Barnes found herself continually in companies involved in technology. She worked at an early version of a company ultimately acquired by Yahoo, spent two years as vice president of sales at Juno Online Services, and then was vice president of business development for several years at Letstalk.com. Ultimately, she became vice president of sales and marketing at Altus Learning Systems, a California-based company that provides archiving and search services for large corporations.

Barnes became a firm practitioner of the "what if" life along the way and has learned the ultimate flexibility when it comes to her career:

I think of myself as a consultant collecting a W2. You can't expect to stay anywhere a long time these days. People hire you to solve the problem, and the problem gets solved. The one constant thing is the customer. I have to remain flexible in my career, but there also is loyalty. My loyalty is to the people, because the company is a thing. You have to know the company isn't loyal to you these days. It's not a cynical view; it's a realistic view. Everyone in the organization services somebody. For example, the HR person has a bottom line, and when you're gone, you're gone.

You have to have your core values and your core strengths. If you do, you can reinvent yourself without angst. I know I'm a salesperson. I can see if wireless or training or the Internet is hot and go there. You can operate yourself like a business. In the old days, when you believed companies had hearts and souls you got burned. Over time you realize everything will be OK. You have to know what you would do if something happens, which can make you constantly slightly paranoid about, say, am I making the bottom line? You have to set the expectations of the person you work for, and you have to have insights into how you want to be compensated. You also have to constantly communicate to management what the customer is going to do. You have to be flexible and faithful to the customer. So if the company suddenly is not faithful to you, are they going to find you your next job? But when you're talking to your potential next employer, the best people for them to talk to are your customers.

This doesn't mean I'm disloyal. I was with one company where I drove the sales from $50,000 to $250,000 in ninety days. They abruptly closed five offices, including mine, around the country and centralized sales in New York. At the time, I took it personally. I was passionate about delivering results for them. My customers were my references.

All partnerships end in death or disillusionment, and working is a partnership. At the end of the day, people care for themselves.

But people will do wonderful things for you, as long as it doesn't hurt them. I'm an extreme case of what can happen.

When you leave your company not of your choosing, the path of least resistance is to go out and find another company that needs help.

It's a disgusting, horrible feeling to feel scared about your job every day. The closer you get to being a complete realist, the better you can handle the event if there is a layoff. You should always have a good résumé ready, go to a lot of industry events, and stay close to your customers. In the old days of doing a résumé, it would be totally factual. Now, it's really a sales document. I view myself as Kim Incorporated, a company of one. Every day I don't count this being where I'm going to work the rest of my life. We are all being forced to be more self-reliant. Work is living together; it's not a marriage.

Employee Loyalty

Employee loyalty just isn't what it used to be. The days of one employee working for one company for an entire career and ultimately retiring from that company, with pride and pension, are, to a great degree, going away. With today's mergers and acquisitions, company closings, downsizing, accounting irregularities, tarnished images, and intense economic pressure on company portfolios and pension plans, an employee is likely to leave with neither pride nor healthy pension, and maybe even a lot sooner than an anticipated retirement.

The larger the company, the more likely there is to be decreasing employee loyalty, according to our surveys of executives and managers. At large companies (those with ten thousand employees or more), employee loyalty is dramatically decreasing, while at small companies, loyalty is actually increasing. At large companies, almost 60 percent of respondents say employees are less loyal than

VOICES FROM THE FRONT LINES:
EMPLOYEE LOYALTY

"Company loyalty has deteriorated significantly from just a generation ago, and that is because the companies have shown they no longer care about their employees (layoffs, no career paths, limited availability of promotion, benefit/pay increases standard instead of those who work really hard being compensated). This has resulted in the employees no longer caring about their employers."

"Turnover of top management erodes employee loyalty. A new executive comes in who knows nothing about the sweat and blood you've shed for the company. They are only concerned with what is your value to me right now."

"With a poor economy and so many reductions in staff, employees are nervous and feel like companies 'don't look after them' as they had in the past."

"It's unfortunate that employee loyalty to the company means little, if anything, anymore. I think our company has suffered greatly (both financially and emotionally) because of the lack of appreciation for employee loyalty."

"Companies seem to have forgotten about compassion and respect. Both can still be realized during difficult economic times. There's been a significant deterioration in how companies treat their employees. Those that have been the worst offenders will pay a dear price when the economy rebounds (which it will) and employment opportunities improve (which will also happen)."

"Loyalty must be honored by both the employee and the employer. There is little loyalty by the latter, which erodes loyalty in employees."

"Salary and compensation issues have diminished in importance generally for many employees. What has become more important are the employer's attitude about the value of employees, the flexibility of employers to grant employees concessions to accommodate personal and family needs, and evidence of empowerment."

"Companies seem to have just completely broken any real sense of trust in the relationship. They confuse the staff by running events that generate loyalty—away days, open door/meet the management, let's all go for an evening out, Christmas dinner together—and then round up their candidates for redundancy the next week. Staff just doesn't believe what management asserts anymore—that 'our people are our best assets'—actually, I think the people are the only asset—try running the company without people. Every piece of behavior seems to tell the staff that management does not think much of them, doesn't trust them, and would happily fire them if they could find a machine to do the job. Staff are getting conflicting signs every day."

"Loyalty is nil, as virtually all employees know that the problem is not the economy or our products but upper management. They listen to the misinformation that is given and understand the whole time it is simply someone attempting to save their own butt at the expense of all others. Why can't the top-level managers see what is so obvious to everyone else?"

"We have put considerable effort into making our company a 'great place to work,' which seems to be paying off. The recession is responsible for some of the improvement in retention, but we give more credit to improvements in employee satisfaction survey results."

"Our company is in the throes of merger, being acquired. General feeling is we were lied to, sold out, and abandoned. 'Only' 20 percent of us are losing our jobs, or as the acquirer is saying, '80 percent' of the jobs are being retained. However, these are mostly the low-paying, clerical, customer service positions. Ah, well, onward to the rest of our lives!"

two years ago. In small companies—those with fewer than a hundred employees—almost half say that loyalty has increased from two years ago, with most of the others saying there was no change. For the most part, the larger the company, the less loyal the employees are, and the smaller the company, the more loyal are the employees.

Bob Yurkovic, formerly director of advanced mobile media at Lucent, spent a total of eighteen years working for Lucent and its predecessor, AT&T. When he started with AT&T, Yurkovic expected he would be with the company for his entire career and then retire, the way it used to be for many.

By 2000, it was apparent that Yurkovic needed to rethink that expectation. Like many companies at the time, Lucent was facing tough market conditions. In mid-2001, thirteen thousand Lucent employees were offered an early-retirement plan, which Yurkovic took. With his experience, Yurkovic expected to relatively quickly land a new position in another company in the New Jersey area, where he lives. "Then 9/11 hit and the telecom market dried up. The recruiters I had talked to even had lost their jobs."

Yurkovic started a company he called Studio IQ, which offered business communication services and created internal corporate radio stations. After several years, Yurkovic decided to head back to the corporate world, though with a different attitude and expectations. Says Yurkovic:

Before, I was looking out for the company. My personal life was second or third in line, after the product and business objectives. My approach was to do whatever it took. Now, I will raise the priority for myself and my family. I can say I would work fewer hours, down to fifty hours rather than the seventy hours a week I worked before. That still involves overtime, but not in a fanatical way. When I have an important event at home, I'll not miss it. I would not be as engaged in a one-sided relationship; my business and personal life would become more balanced.

Anytime you have people churn, it costs money. It always costs more to bring in a new employee, but all the businesses have been trimming expenses way down and sacrificing established, trained personnel. Depleting the workforce of experienced personnel will have long-term effects.

One of the biggest things is that the reasons for staying went away. Unique incentives aren't there anymore, like health care benefits, child care. Even pensions are going away. So what's the reason for loyalty when you can switch companies without losing a thing? Cost cutting and trimming extravagances are necessary when the business faces a downturn, but maintaining some incentive to stay is like adding oil to an engine: it keeps it running efficiently.

I view the company I work for as the hierarchy for command and control, and executives set the ultimate strategy and goals. The president or vice president I work for is the one who would allocate my resources and funding. Focusing on the working environment for my people is key to our success. It's like the air you breathe versus the house you live in . . . a higher priority. Primarily focusing on company facilities and pure numbers causes people to lose faith as they become lower in priority. Executives are in the same boat, and everyone is feeling the same down the line of command. Demoralized, employees let things slip and become frustrated, and the attitude travels further down the chain of command. So, in the end everyone feels that way. Companies shifted focus from people to infrastructure. People are the soul of a company; caring for the people is a requirement for the company's good health. The environment needs to change if a company is to become healthy.

Tough management requires environmental change. People should change jobs (not necessarily companies) at least once every two years. People rise to new challenges more easily than trying to rise to the same challenge month after month. This is one of the reasons companies go outside for managers. Since they have not been bogged down and frustrated by internal battles, outsiders often bring a fresh, exciting, and positive perspective to what has been viewed internally as a staid or static situation.

The workforce of today has different expectations and perhaps a greater perspective and sense of self-confidence within that context.

Joanne Brennan, a former CIO who also led an enterprise-resource-planning (ERP) consulting practice and the IT practice at a finance and IT senior staffing company and who is currently doing independent consulting, says, "If I go back to the corporate world, I would negotiate. I have different ideas today. One of the things I believe in is the mutual benefits of telecommuting. This is different from five years ago. For a long time, I felt compelled to put the company first, and I know that I often shortchanged my family. I reset priorities after 9/11. A lot of our beliefs and priorities changed. I often shortchanged my family in the past."

To attract and keep key people such as Yurkovic and Brennan will require that organizations create an environment in which they and people like them can flourish. It requires a new openness, so that employees, managers, and executives all understand what is expected of them and what they can expect in return.

Improving Employee Loyalty

Here are the top ten solutions for organizations to maintain or improve employee loyalty two years from now, including comments from business executives, based on our research:

1. *Increase confidence in leadership.* Employees want to feel their leaders know where they're going, since the employees have to follow that path. "Confidence in leadership is something you don't hear much about in connection with loyalty. However, if people have confidence in their leaders, they will have confidence in their future."

2. *Improve company culture.* What it's like to work at a company is more important than salary to increase loyalty. This means people need to be treated fairly. "I used to be 100 percent loyal, but now it is everybody for themselves. The current work culture does not encourage loyalty, which adversely affects productivity."

3. *Increase trust.* "Trust is the key issue! The growing gap between executive compensation and what the 'proles' receive does little to increase this. A company with the courage to consciously increase the market value of their staff through training and other means long before the redundancies occur would reap double benefits." Another executive has a similar observation: "It isn't the monetary rewards that build loyalty, it is the feeling of adding value, making a contribution, and being trusted that matter most in building an organization of loyal employees."

4. *Create advancement opportunity.* Employees want to progress. Businesses need to provide a growth path, which becomes increasingly difficult in a shrinking economy.

5. *Promote stability of company.* "In this economy, employees in general do not expect substantial financial increases. Job and company stability and staying power have prominence in most employees' (and managers') minds."

6. *Provide autonomy and challenge.* Provide some tough challenges for employees, and get out of the way! When given the chance, many conscientious employees will rise to a challenge because they desire to make a meaningful contribution.

7. *Provide stability of job.* It's tough to make or get guarantees these days, but job stability stands for a lot when everything else around the employee seems to be changing. "We seem to be losing our younger, promising people due to the extreme demands of a consulting organization. Since we have experienced layoffs in the past two years, their feeling seems to be more of 'Why should I compromise my life when the stability isn't there anymore?'"

8. *Fairly compensate.* In the post-dot-com world, fair pay is expected. Also, managers now prefer performance compensation ahead of equity. "Companies are taking advantage of the unemployment rate by lowering compensation and forcing signing of noncompeting contracts. Loyalty is out the door."

9. *Provide flexibility.* Many are looking for a more balanced life, especially in these trying times.

10. *Monitor benefits.* It's not just the salary that matters for loyalty, there are the other company programs, such as health care coverage, matching company contributions, and employee stock ownership plans, that can more closely link an employee to a company.

Rethinking Retirement Age

On the other side of the issue of company longevity, those who do stay may actually stay longer. Extended life spans, increased health care costs, dwindling investment portfolios, and changing expectations all are driving businesspeople to leave their professional lives later than expected.

Almost half of senior executives and managers plan to retire later than they originally thought. In addition, 80 percent of those who do retire say there is a high probability that they will continue to do additional, paid work. Less than one-fifth of managers see themselves retiring earlier than planned.

People are looking at retirement somewhat differently than their parents did. "I see retirement as a transition, rather than a hard stop," says one manager. "With the downturn in the economy, the investments that would have allowed retirement earlier have diminished dramatically. More important, however, is the fact that I enjoy my work and want to transition into doing things more from the heart but still earning some money."

Unanticipated financial changes also have had an impact on retirement plans. "The rising cost of college for kids, combined

---

SURVEY: RETIREMENT AGE

When do you expect to retire, sooner or later than you originally thought?

Dramatically sooner	5%
Somewhat sooner	13%
When I expected	35%
Somewhat later	38%
Dramatically later	9%

After I retire, the probability that I will continue to do additional paid work is:

Extremely high	32%
Somewhat high	49%
Somewhat low	17%
Extremely low	3%

---

with plunging 401(k)s, has blindsided my retirement planning," says a manager at a medium-sized company. "Oh, well, comfort and security are overrated anyway."

Generational viewpoints and experiences also play a role in future retirement plans, with many taking a highly proactive approach to their future. "Security, whether job, economic, government, or otherwise, no longer exists," says a manager at a large company. "Although I'm only going on thirty, I've already seen multiple iterations of layoffs of employees in their forties and fifties, so I expect zero corporate security. With the way the national debt is piling up and taxes are being reduced, I don't expect Social Security to be around when I retire either, so I am working to create my own financial security."

No matter what stage of their career businesspeople are in, it is time to assess that ultimate, down-the-road decision.

Marian Smithson, a university administrator at Southern Illinois University for the past ten years, recently retired. At sixty-two, she traded her typical sixty-hour workweek for twenty hours as an independent consultant. "I started thinking about it a year and a half in advance," says Smithson. "I was so involved in big issues related to my profession while working full-time that I wanted opportunities to keep my mind sharp after."

Like many in business, Smithson was apprehensive about leaving what seemed so important on a day-to-day basis for the risks associated with heading out on her own, with no corporate family or guaranteed paycheck. "It took about two days to get over it," she says. "Many I know are doing what I'm doing, transitioning and figuring what they want to do next."

With only 3 percent of executives and managers saying that the chances of their doing paid work after retirement is extremely low, it is clear that plans for postretirement are prudent. Retirement should be viewed as a continuing part of the career journey rather than the destination after "work" is complete. It should be viewed more as a time when professional activity will be reduced, not ended.

The large percentage of people who plan to work after their official retirement is not based solely on economic reasons, though it is an obvious factor in today's economy. Like Smithson in Illinois, many simply want to stay engaged.

Professional and Personal Flexibility

Flexibility, in both work and personal life, is a key to tough management. It doesn't mean taking your eye off the ball or deviating from what matters. It does mean a constant reevaluation of what does matter in the context of moving the business forward in step with the overall vision of the organization. To remain flexible today, you must be bold:

- *Try new approaches.* As in the case of Janet Smalley at Marriott, business conditions change, requiring you to adapt to them.

- *Don't rely on old habits.* What worked in the past may—or may not—work now or in the future.
- *Learn from others.* Take a look at peers in another industry. The best lessons often are learned from others in businesses that seemingly have nothing in common with yours.
- *Encourage others to be flexible as well.* Tough management needs to spread to improve overall business success. Train others to move with the punches as you do.

CHAPTER 5

PROVE YOUR VALUE
TO THE COMPANY

Even though most senior executives and managers feel they are more valued today than a few years ago by the people they work for, that value still can be increased. Those who are highly valued are most likely to be the first to be considered for career advancement or some of the company's best new assignments. And during tough times, those who are highly valued will most likely not be the first targets in a corporate downsizing. In addition, increasing and improving value to an organization can increase self-satisfaction, thereby decreasing stress, as discussed in Chapter 4.

The good news is that almost a third of executives and managers feel that they are significantly more valued by their superiors now than a few years ago. "My organization has been excellent at recognizing the value I provide to it, probably more than I do myself," says one manager. "Unfortunately, that isn't true across the board. We seem to have a very whimsical method for deciding who and what brings value to the organization." The latter point is true in many organizations; the most-valued person may be the one who recently made the biggest sale.

Executives and managers have clear ideas on what would increase their value in the eyes of their bosses. Topping the list, perhaps no surprise, is to increase revenue, which gets back to one of the fundamental concepts of tough management: focus on results. There is no more what I call "fluff" left in the work world. The people and departments that deliver results receive the investments and growth opportunities, and that's what tough management is all about.

Aligning with Your Company's Value

To increase your value inside your organization, tough management requires that you align with the real value of what your business provides, which means identifying the true value of what your business does. This requirement does not refer to a technical definition of *value*, which is the monetary worth or fair market price of something. Rather, what value does your business provide to its customers and stakeholders?

While most companies tout customer service, their internal measurement systems often are based on products sold, not necessarily on customers satisfied. Granted, some companies reward managers for customer satisfaction levels or use balanced scorecards, but generally "units sold" or "revenue produced" dominates overall compensation or, at the very least, internal recognition of who is king (or queen) of the hill.

Companies historically were organized around the design of products, often to the point that entire groups or divisions would focus on creating and marketing single categories of products. Companies then would organize to sell these products to a designated market of buyers, typically with the biggest buyers receiving the most attention. Some of the largest companies with many products, such as IBM, organized sales forces around industries and lined up the various product groups necessary to support that industry.

The world is different today, with all product and pricing information available to all through the networking of everything, with accessibility primarily through the Internet. This networking of everything created a new dilemma for the makers of products.

With instant access to all information all the time, buyers instantly measure supply against demand, price against price, and feature against feature. (Anyone who has ever used eBay can see how markets and pricing work in a real-time world.)

We are going through a value shift, where companies can find that their core assets are less profitable or less well positioned for the future than what surrounds and supplements the actual product. This shift can affect just about any product, from hard to soft goods. An obvious example is real-time stock quotes. They used to be available only to brokers charged a large fee by the New York Stock Exchange. For consumers, the standard monthly fee used to be $29.95 for information that is now free. Likewise, real estate listings used to be available only through a broker; now they're available on the Net. Service contracts at Circuit City account for all of its operating profit, and almost half at BestBuy. In these cases, the core assets—electronics—are less valuable to the bottom line of the organization than are the service contracts, which surround those products.

Tough management requires identifying these shifts within your organization and aligning with where the value is and where it is going. It is common knowledge that making and selling a product is no longer enough, even at a competitive price. The value is in tying together everything a company has to offer and essentially wrapping that offering around the customer, as many companies have come to realize.

What some companies still fail to see is that from their customers' viewpoint, their products, services, and brands are viewed as one entity. For example, customers want a bank to know who they are. But instead, one bank employee knows they have a checking account, another knows they have a savings account, and a third person knows they have a mortgage. The bank might be organized around its products, which is how many companies grew up.

Many businesses started with a core product and evolved from there. Typically, a product was created. When it succeeded or failed, another product was created. The company ended up with many potentially very good products. However, it might have no organization around the buyers of all those products.

As departments and companies determine what true value they provide as viewed through the eyes of their customers, this presents an opportunity for you to align with those same values. Start by asking these questions:

- What services does the customer appreciate?
- How do the best customers view the company?
- What is lacking?
- What is internal business development working on?
- What did we just launch?
- What brings in the most revenue?

The answers to these questions force an organization to focus more on customer needs than on internal issues. The key to proving value to your company is to align yourself with the values of the company itself. For example, if there is a big cost-cutting push on, lead the charge, and make sure the top brass knows it. This may sound heartless, but the reality is if there is across-the-board cutting, you'll be affected anyway. If it's the last quarter and all eyes are on making the revenue numbers, make sure you are prominent in that charge. It is essential to have the value you provide aligned with the values the company provides.

Top Ten Ways to Be More Valued by Your Organization (in Order)
1. Increase revenue
2. Do more with less
3. Increase profit
4. Communicate more
5. Cut costs
6. Provide creative ideas
7. Assume more responsibility
8. Collaborate more
9. Share more information
10. Spend more time with customers

Value: Selling What You Can't See

As you attempt to align with your business's value, it is also important to assess the less tangible parts of the value. For example, in these tougher times, there is great opportunity for businesses to sell things that can't be seen. Consumers around the world in one year spent $3.5 billion for cell-phone ring tones. More than $1 trillion was spent for insurance, including accident, health, and property. The point is there is tremendous revenue in things that you can't see.

One of the primary reasons is that the pricing for invisible products is more difficult to evaluate. For example, a manufacturer can determine how much it costs to make a DVD player, based on the cost of the components and the labor to make it. Based on profit margins, it is relatively straightforward to determine the cost of the product to the distributor, who in turn can properly price it for the consumer. Competitors can easily calculate those same costs, and competition continually drives those prices down by decreasing production costs and profit margins.

This has been the basic measurement system for hard goods for decades. For a while, the Internet challenged all those assumptions with market valuations based on futures, which were not necessarily based on anything, since the territory was so uncharted.

SURVEY: **VALUE PROVIDED**

When it comes to the value I provide to my department/ organization, I feel that today I am valued by my superiors:

Significantly more than a few years ago	29%
Somewhat more than a few years ago	38%
The same	16%
Somewhat less than a few years ago	13%
Significantly less than a few years ago	4%

However, aside from the Net, selling what cannot be seen can be a great business. The selling of "invisibles" falls into one of five categories:

1. *Peace of mind.* Customers buy peace of mind in the form of service contracts and extended warranties. After you buy that expensive sound system at Best Buy, do you really want to take a chance on it breaking two years down the road? Under this category falls the brand itself. Companies buy from IBM, Dell, etc., because they perceive that the companies will stand behind the products. That is the value of the brand and the market position of a company. This intangible of brand causes sales of those companies' products. Insurance also falls under this category, as people feel better that they are "covered." The same holds true for security monitoring services.

2. *Futures.* Cell phone services are a great example of buying what we loosely refer to as futures, as people pay for a future amount of time per month. People are paying for something they plan to use later. Advertisers buy future advertising time on television, and people purchase future time-shares for properties.

3. *Rights.* Cable and satellite television fees allow consumers the right to see certain programming. For extra charges, people can have more rights to see more things.

4. *Ideas.* Examples of the selling of ideas are portrayed in consulting or paid advice, as the pricing of intellectual property is market driven.

5. *Dreams.* There is the dream of winning the lottery or investing in the results of a future event, such as gambling that the next roulette number will be yours.

Businesses sometimes miss providing customers with some of these intangibles and lose sight of what they think they are selling versus what someone feels they are buying. Tough management means adding some intangibles to the selling of hard goods. One

"Unfortunately, management value today is relegated to a person's ability to increase revenue and decrease costs. It seems as if leadership, compassion and fairness with employees, and ability to keep the business moving in the right direction isn't enough anymore. It's about profits. You don't make enough, you're not valued."

"I provide IT solutions to our department's business processes. As I have come up with more, they have grown to rely on it more. They now see the potential that things like centralized data can provide, and they have become intoxicated by the possibilities. There just are not the hours in the day to keep up with the demand."

"Company recently acquired, so value proposition changed dramatically—challenged to integrate into a vastly different business culture (much smaller). Downsizing spans both organizational and technological dimensions. New owner is focused on metrics that have little to do with previous value of the position. Bottom line is that while I still believe that the value is there, just no way to have it register at this point in time."

"I am a small contractor, and I am finding that those companies hiring my services want more from me, usually ASAP, but definitely drag their feet in paying my invoices in a timely matter or sometimes not at all. I am hearing similar complaints from other small contractors about not being paid."

"Information technology has become so critical that it is managed by businesspeople that don't understand enough to make good IT decisions. My superiors just do not have the background to value my contributions. They do have enough business sense to understand that I do something essential to their survival."

"We are currently living in a period of doing more with less. I have just joined a new employer, and my focus is to find ways to improve the company at the lowest cost possible. New ideas are valued more, since management skills are expected from you."

"I probably do more than the overall organization is aware; if this were self-promoted, it would lead to additional recognition of my value to the organization."

way is to provide the peace of mind that the company will back its product in the future, no matter what the warranty says. Another is to provide great customer service, showing customers that if they conduct business with you, they will be well treated all the time. In many cases, it is the service that matters more to the buyer than the product itself.

The bottom line is that the five categories of peace of mind, futures, rights, ideas, and dreams all come under the category of value. Though cell-phone rings, insurance, and warranties can't be seen, they have a real value in the mind of the buyer. So businesses should analyze the true value of what they provide to customers and business partners and how they might provide more of it.

Aligning yourself with the value your business provides its customers may sound like being an opportunist, but the reality is that the alignment will not only be good for you, but also good for the organization because you will focus on what matters to the organization most at any given time.

Adding Value by Accepting Challenge

Another way to increase your value inside your organization is to take on and delegate some healthy challenges. The majority of senior executives and managers around the world already feel

---

SURVEY: CHALLENGE

In my current position, I generally feel:

Very challenged	52%
Somewhat challenged	39%
Not very challenged	7%
Not at all challenged	2%

Employees and/or managers who ultimately report to me are:

Very challenged	48%
Somewhat challenged	50%
Not very challenged	3%
Not at all challenged	0%

---

somewhat challenged in their current positions. More than 90 percent say they are either very or somewhat challenged, with more than half saying they are very challenged.

These business leaders also appear to be passing on some of their demands to others. Ninety-seven percent say that the employees or managers who ultimately report to them are either very or somewhat challenged.

People in business are facing two types of challenges:

1. *Pressure to perform because of external forces.* These forces can originate externally but have workload implications on any given business. "We are challenged with constantly changing environments, tasks, and duties in the current economic environment that forces organizations to cut back on people and increase workloads for their existing employees," says one manager at a small company. "And as the old adage goes, the better you are at doing your job, the more they give you to do." A senior executive at a medium-sized company says, "The most

challenging task is to manage large amounts of work with a small staff in the time allotted."

2. *Pressure from within the company itself.* This internal pressure can come from managers or coworkers who don't have the same attitude about a task at hand. "The challenging part for us is not the job, because we thrive on job/task challenges, but some of the people internally with whom we must deal," says a man-

---

VOICES FROM THE FRONT LINES: CHALLENGE

"I am always challenged, working to deadlines, negotiating hard deals, etc., but what I lack is creative license."

"The only challenge I face is learning how to work without a challenge until I find a company that can challenge me."

"My role is new-business development, which is always difficult. These challenges are increased when the financial results for existing businesses are below expectations and new business growth isn't great enough to offset the shortfall."

"My organization is continuing to invest in technology to develop and deliver knowledge management. With a multimillion-dollar commitment from the board of directors and a very high expectation from the same, I expect to have plenty of challenges for the near future."

"I think the challenges are above what most of our people can do. In some cases, this will cause people to burn out and leave. A lot of stress and burnout due to unrealistic expectations."

"The challenges are twofold. First, there is the responsibility to manage more tasks with fewer dollars. The second is to rise above the competition and perform at a higher level than anybody else. The challenge is not in figuring out the answers. It is coming up with the questions."

ager at a small company. Pressures cause people to dig deep and stretch to meet a goal or expectation, which can be very healthy. "People are motivated more by a challenging job than money," says a senior executive at a small company. "Creating a challenging work environment is one of the most important tasks of a manager, and one of the most difficult."

Challenges drive a business and can make it an exciting place to be. People should be challenged in good times as well as in not-so-good times. Creating challenge in an organization can cause people to deliver what might appear to someone else as being beyond their reach. Tough management requires that you seek out new challenges because they are what will drive the business forward in the future. By associating yourself with these challenges, you will increase your focus to more of what matters most to the business at the time.

Stretching the Workforce

There is a fine line between proving your value to the organization and having that organization take advantage of the great value you provide. Work today is much more of a two-way street. The employer-employee "contract" is different than in the past. Leaders of organizations sometimes lose sight of this by overlooking the details of what their managers and workers face at work on a day-to-day basis.

With tight budgets and cost cutting, employee payroll is closely monitored at many businesses, and any opportunity where an executive can save even a few weeks can seem appealing. This can lead to what I call "stretching the workforce," where executives tap current managers or workers to temporarily fill in for coworkers who are out for whatever reason—vacation, temporary leave, or whatever. The danger in stretching the workforce arises when company leaders take advantage of situations and current staffers and make the process of the stretch too long.

Kate M. is a licensed practical nurse at a Massachusetts-area assisted-living practice that is part of a national assisted-living company. Kate, who has worked there for four years, following eight years on the staff of a nursing home, has been part of a stretched workforce.

Kate joined the company as program director of the facility's special-care unit. The organization's six departments—special care, nursing, maintenance, activities, food service, and the business office—each have a department head, and these managers report to an executive director. The special-care unit generally houses twenty-four residents, all of whom have Alzheimer's disease or dementia, which Kate has been trained to handle. In addition, the facility rents forty-five apartments to residents whose needs are handled by the nursing department.

In both the nursing and special-care departments, the nurses serve the needs of the patients or residents, from coordinating with families and support groups to coordinating medical needs and staff scheduling. Says Kate:

For the first three years that I worked there, there were two people who worked in special care and nursing. When the nursing manager quit for a position elsewhere, a replacement was hired. That person left after one day on the job, once she determined that the on-call hours would be too much. The executive director asked me to fill in for two weeks, and that was four months ago. This is the fifth time this has happened to me at this organization in three and a half years. I receive no extra pay, and I have mentioned it a few times. I keep telling them that one person doing both can do neither job correctly. Sometimes they complain to me about things not getting done. They say, "I know you're doing two jobs, but . . ." I could say I'll only do one job, but then the forty-five people would have no one to help. I could go to the executive director and say I won't do both jobs anymore, but she'd probably say, "Hang in there." As long as you're willing to wear ten hats, they'll let you wear ten hats.

Kate says the organization has been slow in interviewing and hiring. "They don't force the hard decisions," she says. "They let the applications pile up for three weeks before looking at them." So how do people like Kate become part of the stretched workforce? Kate describes her point of view:

I said no and got stuck with it anyway. You just can't turn your back on the residents. They know you're not going to just ignore the residents; it's not in your character.

No doesn't really mean no, though I think I'll mean it more next time. I believe in what we do and that assisted living is the best thing to come down the pike in a long time.

I think that in health care, they're always looking to ask you to do more, because the professionals don't want to jeopardize the care of the people you're taking care of.

I'm not bitter, but I am frustrated. The executive directors generally are businesspeople, not health care people. They're held accountable for revenue and earnings, and we're held accountable for occupancy as well as health care. Ours don't conflict, because if we find someone who needs assisted living rather than a nursing home, you really are providing a better quality of life.

During my summer vacation, I was temporarily replaced by two nurses from another assisted-living center that is part of the company. After vacation, there will be a lot to catch up on. I like the work that I do, but things could be a lot better, such as paying people for what they're worth when they can afford it. Still, I can't do both jobs well for months at a time.

I used to love going to work every day. Now, I walk in and know there will be chaos until I walk out the door. There is way too much stress. You really have to fight for your personal life.

So while tough management requires that you prove your value to the organization, it also mandates that you watch out for yourself in the process. While you look for new ways to provide value to the organization, you also should be looking for how the organization provides value to you.

Different Values at Different Times

When it comes to internal alignment of the appropriate value you provide, it is important to understand what your superiors value and where your experiences might match those values. It's no secret that many in business behave differently at different stages of their careers. People with more experience may make decisions based on their experiences, while those with less experience may tend to take more risks, based on simple lack of seeing potential downsides. However, once older (and presumably wiser), many can look through their business lives and easily identify characteristics with certain levels of work experience.

Different characteristics seem to be most pronounced at certain stages of a person's career, at least from one group's viewpoint. We asked senior executives and managers to identify which characteristics were most likely to be found in people closest to ages 22, 32, 42, 52, and 62. As might be expected, the overwhelming majority (94 percent) of respondents, being in management positions, were in the age groups closest to 42, 52, and 62, so the results are effectively the view of businesspeople closest to those ages, not necessarily of all people in business. Here's what they said:

- Those who are closest to 52 years old were perceived to be the most balanced, knowledgeable about business, loyal, thankful and appreciative, trustworthy, willing to teach, and willing to share.
- Those closest to age 62 were perceived to be the most likely to be conservative and knowledgeable about life.
- Those closest to age 22 were perceived to be the most fun, technologically adept, willing to learn, and willing to travel.

A more interesting way to look at the issue is by characteristic. Here are the characteristics, followed by the ages chosen most often and second most often:

- Aggressive: those closest to age 32, 22
- Balanced: 52, 42
- Conservative: 62, 52
- Family oriented: 42, 32
- Fun: 22, 32
- Knowledgeable about business: 52, 32
- Knowledgeable about life: 62, 52
- Loyal: 52, 62
- Open: 42, 22
- Technologically adept: 22, 32
- Thankful/appreciative: 52, 62
- Trustworthy: 52, 42
- Willing to change: 32, 22
- Willing to learn: 22, 32
- Willing to teach: 52, 42
- Willing to travel: 22, 32
- Willing to share: 52, 62

There are obvious factors that determine the reason some of these characteristics are associated with certain ages. Those factors include economic conditions and particular business or industry situation.

"Some of these characteristics, such as willing[ness] to travel, are true for the younger and older, while others are not age dependent," says one manager (who is closest to age 52). "Personally, I have a broader business base in my fifties and was most loyal at 40, before major organization restructuring/sale, so these are also situational. Generally, good employees only get better unless there are adverse personal circumstances, and I find real strong career

SURVEY: AGE CHARACTERISTICS

Based on your experience, the following characteristics are most likely to be found in persons closest to which age in business today:

	Age				
	22	**32**	**42**	**52**	**62**
Base	16.1%	18.5%	20.8%	26.0%	15.6%
Aggressive	26%	55%	13%	3%	0%
Balanced	0%	2%	29%	59%	8%
Conservative	2%	2%	12%	32%	51%
Family oriented	1%	20%	56%	15%	6%
Fun	48%	29%	10%	6%	2%
Knowledgeable about business	0%	5%	32%	48%	14%
Knowledgeable about life	0%	0%	8%	40%	50%
Loyal	1%	4%	18%	46%	28%
Open	24%	22%	27%	16%	8%
Technologically adept	45%	41%	8%	3%	1%
Thankful/appreciative	4%	9%	20%	39%	26%
Trustworthy	2%	6%	26%	38%	23%
Willing to change	28%	42%	19%	5%	2%
Willing to learn	39%	37%	12%	6%	3%
Willing to teach	1%	8%	30%	40%	17%
Willing to travel	48%	22%	16%	8%	2%
Willing to share	4%	11%	20%	37%	26%

commitment tends to come in the late twenties and early thirties, often in conflict with family demands."

Many factors influence these characteristics, such as background, training, attitude, and upbringing. For example, a fun person at 22 can still be fun at 52, and a person can be trustworthy (or not) for an entire career. Also, if an age group has a certain characteristic, it may not be the same for every person in that age group. "My mentor was a very gifted fifty-something, while the other fifty-somethings that I work with tend to be turf-sensitive and manipulative," says one respondent (closest to age 42).

The business reality is that no matter the characteristic at a given age, everyone in a department or a company has to interact with those in different groups with different characteristics. The key is to leverage all the positive attributes across the enterprise and link the knowledge in those who are most experienced, who say they are the most willing to share, with those in the youngest groups, who are identified as the most willing to learn.

Top Executive Skills

To improve your value, tough management requires focusing on mastering those skills that will matter most for future success. For example, communicating well is critical both now and in the future, as discussed in Chapter 1. But focus, collaboration, and perspective also are important, all selected by a large majority of senior executives and managers as the skills most important to be successful.

SURVEY: EXECUTIVE SKILLS

For the executive and manager of today to be successful, which of the following skills are the most important?

Ability to:

Communicate well	94%
Stay focused	77%
Collaborate with others	74%
Keep overall perspective	68%
Learn	64%
Prioritize tasks	64%
Plan	62%
Manage external relations	60%
Manage internal relations	57%

continued

Manage time	52%
Assess competition	51%
Organize	50%
Meet deadlines	49%
Teach	47%
Direct others	46%
Handle customer issues	45%
Use technology	41%
Be personable	39%
Manage others	39%
Deploy technology	35%

For the executive and manager of tomorrow to be successful, which of the following skills will be the most important?

Ability to:

Communicate well	88%
Stay focused	79%
Collaborate with others	73%
Keep overall perspective	66%
Learn	63%
Plan	62%
Prioritize tasks	61%
Assess competition	58%
Manage external relations	57%
Use technology	56%
Manage internal relations	56%
Teach	52%
Manage time	50%
Organize	50%
Deploy technology	47%
Handle customer issues	47%
Meet deadlines	45%
Direct others	40%
Manage others	39%
Be personable	35%

Working Away from the Office

Tough management means that proving your value to your superiors should be based on what you deliver, not on how many hours you work or even where you work, for that matter. The reality is that executives and managers are spending more time working away from the office, which for the most part, has made their lives better. Working away from the office can provide more thinking time, more perspective, and even more time to focus on what values at your company you should be aligning with. The trend of spending more time working at home is being driven by several factors, including work overload and desire for increased productivity:

- Sixty-one percent of senior executives and managers say the amount of time they have spent working out of the office (telecommuting, home office, etc.) has increased over the last three years.
- Only 9 percent say their amount of time working away from the office has decreased.
- Almost half say it has made their life overall either extremely or somewhat better (18 percent say it is worse).

Whether or not people want to work more at home is almost academic, as the harsh business realities of today drive it. Many people take work home because it's physically impossible to get it all done during the normal workday. "The workload has increased considerably at the office, without increasing staff," says one manager at a medium-sized company. "This has caused me to spend considerably more time working from my home office, which started as a convenience and now is a necessity."

Says a manager at a small company, "With the economy in such a downturn the past few years, a heavy burden has been placed on managers to pick up the workload. Managers can stay at the office until the middle of the night or take the work home. The advantage is at least you are at home. The disadvantage is you really

"With the increase in e-mail and voice-mail volume (every message is a project!), managers oftentimes find themselves filled with more work. Thus, whether you're at home or work, there isn't much free time to enjoy 'time away.'"

"While there is certainly some flexibility and convenience by being able to conduct business from home or away from the office, it has dramatically increased the amount of time I work. I have had to develop more disciplined work habits; otherwise I would never turn off work mode."

"I find that, to stay up on things, I have to work at home in the evenings just to stay ahead of e-mails, etc. Cell phones and Blackberries also make me always available and pretty much on call twenty-four hours a day."

"Working from home allows an employee the needed flexibility to fit work and life together. Being part of a team connected electronically is a new definition of community. Companies can expand their access to expertise, reduce working stress, and increase productivity in a well-thought-out electronic workplace."

"Today's reduced staffing requires that I be more available to coworkers. Thus, working from home has become a luxury we can't afford."

"Working out of the office substantially improves my life quality. Once in a while it allows me to work wearing just my pajamas."

"Working from my home office has not only made me more productive, but has enabled me to create more balance in my life. Even just simple things like mowing the lawn during a lunch break can be empowering. It has also made globalization easier because I can do off-time-zone meetings from the comfort of my home office after homework, dinner, bedtime stories, etc."

"The line between work and family is becoming blurred. With PDAs forwarding e-mails, cell phones, and voice mail, it is great to have instant access to the office, but it begins to invade the personal side of our lives."

"Closing regional sales offices and having the salesmen work from their homes is our trend. Saves some cost, but you lose intercommunication. We'll see down the road the real cost of this move."

"Overall, I am more productive in a home office. Few distractions, less stress, no office politics, etc. It's nice to get up and read the paper, have coffee, and walk over to the office and look out the window at the oak tree in my front yard. Especially with teleconferencing and Webcast, there is little reason to have to travel to the corporate office more than once a quarter. I get paid or not paid based on quantitative results. At the end of the day, that's what matters."

"The flexibility of being able to manage from anywhere is extremely useful. I can be at my second home, in China, Taiwan, or anyplace and still manage my department or get projects completed. When I want to be totally away on vacation, I can elect not to take along the computer, cell phone, e-mail, etc."

"I've been surprised how much more efficient it is working from a well-designed and equipped home office than from my usual office. Instant access is sacrificed, but more work is accomplished because of fewer unnecessary interruptions. The downside is you don't run into people to discuss topical items and get quick updates."

"Technology has made it easier to do things away from the office. That is the good and the bad news. While at times it helps with the work/family balance, I find myself working more total hours because the technology enables it."

"Over the past few years, we have re-created our office systems so that our consultants can work remotely. On the upside, we can work twenty-four hours a day wherever we are. On the downside, see the upside."

aren't spending any quality time with your family. Sadly, top exec-utives are becoming comfortable with the leaner staff, and the work is still getting done."

The business pressures of the past several years have spread throughout organizations, with the workload never decreasing and layoffs leaving workers left behind to work even harder. "I tend to work seven days a week, although the time per day varies from ten to twelve hours during the week to two to six hours per day on week-ends," says a senior executive at a medium-sized company. "It's hard to imagine my job getting more intense."

Survival Tips for Working Away from the Office

- *Be disciplined.* One of the main reasons to work away from the office is to get more done. Focus on getting it done, and don't drag it out.
- *Remain visible.* The adage "out of sight, out of mind" applies. Those who work at home can make easier targets as downsizing candidates.
- *Check in with peers.* Coworkers might think you're taking it easy at home, though you're working seven days a week. Make sure they have a feel for what you're up to.
- *Use commute time.* If you're saving an hour or two a day by not commuting to the office, make sure you use that extra time to full advantage.
- *Disconnect.* Whether working at home or at the office, it's still working. Give yourself a break.
- *Measure productivity.* Determine when you are most productive when working away from the office, and maximize those periods.
- *Be creative.* Use the time away from the office as a time of not only increased productivity, but also increased creativity.
- *Take time to think.* This can give you a broader perspective, which can help you in tackling issues back at the office, thereby increasing the value you provide.

Working away from the office also can cause a sense of isolationism. Wayne Daigle, an independent consultant, left an office-based position several years ago and now can play catch with his three-year-old son between meetings. However, the challenge he and others face is to avoid working too long alone in a home office with decreasing interaction with associates. "At times it can get lonely, but being around to see my children grow up is well worth it," says Daigle. However, some time spent working away from the office can improve balance, which many business environments are sorely lacking today.

If done right, working away from the office can allow you to be more productive with fewer distractions and more focused on adding true value to your business.

On the Road to Work

With the workday getting longer, tougher, and filled with distractions and interruptions, tough management means that businesspeople have to move some of their thinking time to the commute to and from work. The majority of senior executives and managers spend more than a half hour commuting daily, and a third spend an hour or more. And the larger the company, the longer the commute time: 15 percent of management in companies with more than ten thousand employees spends two hours or more a day commuting.

With the eight-hour day having been replaced by days of nine, ten, or more hours, part of work is being shifted to commute time out of necessity. "The hour and fifteen minutes I spend commuting is therapeutic," says one manager at a medium company. "It allows me to prepare for the working day on the way in and unwind on the way home." Says a senior executive at a large company, "I use my commuting time preparing for my day in the morning and trying to decompress in the evening."

SURVEY: **COMMUTING TIME**

On a typical workday, I spend the following total amount of time daily commuting to and from work:

0–30 minutes	37%
31–60 minutes	29%
1–2 hours	25%
2–3 hours	6%
3–4 hours	2%
4–5 hours	0%
5 hours or more	0%

Commuting time is affected by geography and proximity to the workplace as well as by lifestyle decisions. "After September 11, I made a decision to live close to work and commute by walking from my condo to the office," says one senior executive at a medium-sized company who moved from New York to a condo in Philadelphia, with a home in Hilton Head, South Carolina. Says a senior executive in a small company, "I'm fortunate to live in the Twin Cities, with good bus service between my home in the suburbs and office in downtown Minneapolis."

Some live close enough to the office to avoid driving altogether. "I have the wonderful situation of living in downtown Chicago and walking to work," says a senior executive in a small company. "It takes me fifteen to twenty minutes each way, and the walking has done wonders for weight management and overall health. The walk is invigorating and helps me get ready for the day, and to unwind after work. If more CEOs could do this, it would help us all."

The time to and from work can be used for work- and non-work-related activities. In fact, 74 percent of executives and managers spend their commuting time listening to the radio and recordings of music or educational and entertainment program-

"With so many cutbacks in personnel over the past few years, what used to be a relaxing commute has become additional work time. The advantage, of course, [is that] you can finalize or begin things you didn't have an opportunity to do while officially at work. It relieves some of the stress of the overload of work and the pressure that comes in today's job."

"A fifteen-minute commute each way increases productivity and satisfaction enormously while reducing stress."

"I drive to work, so listening to the radio and thinking [are] the only real options. I don't use a cell phone while driving at all (e.g., no hands-free, etc.). I'll use the drive in to work to prep for the day and the drive home to decompress."

"I can review e-mail on a Blackberry at stoplights and can use a cell phone to check messages while driving."

"With a smaller management team, my Blackberry and cell phone have made my commuting time a necessary (but at least convenient) extension of my workday."

"Commuting by car limits my ability to accomplish anything beyond phone calls. Having said that, I'm amazed by the number of people I see reading while driving! Yet another example of the suicidal behavior of Atlanta motorists!"

"Long commutes are both a pain and benefit. Although I get up at 4:00 A.M. to take the 6:00 A.M. train and get home about 7:30 P.M. (except for client dinner nights), the existence seems reasonable. When I think about it, though, it is insane."

"Although I do not have a long way to travel to work, the time traveling I consider being work time. From the moment I get into the car, my mind turns to my day, and I am thinking and organizing. Normally, as soon as one arrives at work, it is hard to find a few minutes when you are not fully engaged in decisions and demands. Travel time is one of my most productive thirty minutes during the day."

ming. "I spend almost all my time in the car listening to business and personal development tapes or CDs," says one senior executive at a small company. "There is so much information that I can absorb, it seems that I get a class a day in, which adds up to a great education."

However, more than half of senior executives and managers spend their commute time thinking, the highest time use after listening to the radio. Thinking during the commute provides yet another way to conceive of innovations that increase your value to the business. Rachel Radwinsky, a vice president at Merrill Lynch in New Jersey, commutes three hours a day. She spends the time catching up with family on the phone, listening to audiobooks and the radio, and thinking productively. "The thinking time is very good when there is no traffic," she says. "I come up with some of my better thoughts on how to solve problems at work while commuting." So whether your daily commute is a few minutes or a few hours, it can be used for a thinking moment, which might help solve a business problem or just provide fresh perspective to the day ahead.

What Executives and Managers Do While Commuting to Work (in Order)

1. Listen to radio
2. Think
3. Use a phone
4. Relax
5. Work
6. Read

Add Value, Be Flexible, and Collaborate

Once your superiors understand how the value you provide is aligned with the value the business is attempting to provide, your worth to the organization will rise. By taking on more challenges in areas that are the most important to the business, you increase your value even more. But, as detailed in Chapter 4, it also is important to remain flexible so that the value you provide can shift as those that the company provides move with markets.

Tough management requires that you try to work away from the office more, where you can keep perspective of what matters most. It also means taking time to think, whether while commuting or during some other off time, because once you enter the heads-down treadmill at the office, it can be easy to lose overall perspective. And once the value you provide is aligned with the values that the business provides, it becomes easier to collaborate with others internally, as discussed in the next chapter.

CHAPTER 6

FORCE
COLLABORATION

Tough management requires teamwork. Collaboration at every level of the organization is the key for executives and managers, who see collaborating with others as a critical skill to succeed. (Collaboration is rated more important by twice as many executives and managers as is managing others or being personable.) Working with others is becoming so important because of the increasing complexity of work itself. With the economic and competitive pressures, companies have been seeking ways to increase productivity by increasing efficiency as well as revenue, making for a more integrated approach to solving problems.

Businesses also have been turning to technology to help increase collaboration. Tech tools such as videoconferencing and real-time and work group collaboration software are on the increase. GE even created an online program that allows up to three participants to doodle illustrations simultaneously on the same Web page while communicating through chat during the process. The first time GE tried a similar but less interactive program, six million sketches were e-mailed within 140 countries. Research firm Gartner shows that the market for real-time collaboration software grew by 30 percent in one year recently, with the expectation that within a few years, 60 percent of Fortune 2000 companies will be using Web conferencing companywide.

The good news for businesses of all sizes is that collaboration and teamwork are being taught and emphasized at business schools across the country. From the first day at the Anderson School of Management at the University of California–Los Angeles (UCLA), teamwork is an integral part of everyday life. On the East Coast, the Wharton School at the University of Pennsylvania and the Whittemore School of Business and Economics at the University of New Hampshire both stress teams in their curricula, with Wharton deploying a laboratory in collaborative leadership.

Tough management requires collaborating with others on common business goals, which can improve a person's ability to create work relationships and better utilize those relationships and view them as critical resources. A manager describes the need this way: "Resource management, internal and external, may be the single most important skill that executives and managers must possess in the future—where and how to find the information that you need to get the job done. Who knows? And who knows who knows? That requires both energy management and networking skills to establish and manage relationships. Managing relationships is resource management."

Managing relationships is a critical factor in successful collaboration and teamwork. Another great advantage of collaboration is that participants come to understand human resistance issues and learn to deal with them at all levels. Collaboration effectively causes people to agree on common goals and to focus their energies on those goals, fulfilling one of the key rules of tough management: focus on results. Successfully working in a team environment requires give-and-take, but it also allows individuals the opportunity to learn and grow.

Every member of a team has something to contribute, and every other member has something to learn. Organizations that encourage collaboration with highly interactive participation by all team members can provide that organization with a great advantage of focusing all energies in an agreed-to direction. The problem is that many organizations talk about collaboration and say they believe in it, but don't take the right steps to make true teamwork work for the good of the organization.

Forcing Collaboration Through Priority Thinking

The MasterCraft Boat Company is located in Venore, Tennessee, a relatively short drive from Knoxville. Anyone who water-skis or wakeboards is familiar with the MasterCraft brand, since boats the company produces are used in every major ski show and water-ski and wakeboard tournament, often televised. MasterCraft is also the market leader in dollar volume in its category, with almost 25 percent market share of all inboard ski boats sold. The thirty-seven-year-old company, which has 550 employees, sells its boats through a network of 125 dealers.

When John Dorton took over as president and CEO in 1999, the company had $56 million annual revenue but was losing money. By 2004, company revenue had risen to $128 million with no debt and earnings of roughly 10 percent. MasterCraft tops its category in market share by dollar volume, with a 30 percent lead over its closest competitor. Ironically, the boats are also the most expensive ski and wakeboard boats, so the company has to continually rethink how it works.

Dorton reasoned that the only way to become highly efficient while continuing to drive higher-quality products and innovation was to force total internal collaboration. Another reason for requiring more collaboration was that managers seemed to be working harder and harder but weren't getting any more done in line with company objectives.

"Our concept was that you could fill your day up with duties and focus on what is urgent to the business," says Dorton. "It was clear that the managers would float through the day and be very busy and feel like they got a lot done. They were busy, but were they busy on the right things?"

Dorton discussed this concept of working on the right thing with the executive team on many occasions, and they generally agreed it would be a better approach. "They would agree we needed to do it, but it never progressed."

Dorton determined that he had to realign the mind-set. He assembled the leadership team, including the heads of sales, marketing, manufacturing, engineering, and HR. Over the course of one and a half months, they drafted the following vision statement, to which they all agreed:

> *By July 1, 2007, MasterCraft Boat Company will be the world's leading luxury performance inboard sport boat designer and builder in quality and unit and dollar volume. Consumers will rate the MasterCraft dealer experience in the top two of J. D. Powers. The company will reduce its dependency on wholesale push and be driven by retail demand. We will greatly improve the speed of our supply chain to respond to this retail demand through the aggressive application of lean and Six Sigma thinking, IT initiatives and tools in every area of our business. Our employees will be passionate about our products, self-directed, and empowered to make improvements to satisfy and make the customer a success. Our company will be a very safe, friendly, fair, open, and accountable work culture that seeks and achieves high performance in everything we do. As a result, we will increase shareholder value.*

Once the statement was completed, the team broke it into separate elements that could be measured:

- Greatest quality, most units, and highest dollar volume among the world's designers and builders of luxury performance inboard sport boats
- The company will reduce its dependency on wholesale push and be driven by retail demand.

- First- or second-place rating of the MasterCraft dealer experience in consumer ratings reported by J. D. Powers
- Greatly improved speed of the supply chain resulting from aggressive application of lean and Six Sigma thinking
- IT initiatives and tools deployed in every area of the business
- Employees passionate about MasterCraft products, self-directed, and empowered to make improvements to satisfy and make the customer a success
- Unanimous employee rating of the company as having a very safe, friendly, fair, open, and accountable work culture that seeks and achieves high performance in all its activities

The company wanted to link or map each item to other items, showing the interdependence of each. So the company listed each of the modules, the elements just mentioned, to a MasterCraft Strategy Map, separating the elements that pertained to growth from those that dealt with productivity. The difference between top-line growth and cost reduction became obviously clear. It was then relatively straightforward to determine what tactics or activities would be required for each module and who would be responsible for each. The most significant change inside the company, however, was that each person responsible for any given area could plainly see the implications of tactics in other areas affecting them, and vice versa. Says Dorton:

> *We all agreed on the mission statement and came out with seven or eight pieces, all clusters. Each represented a significant piece to the vision puzzle. We then said you would have to spend a day or a week or ninety minutes a day delivering this. It was used to help people understand how their life affects someone else's. It took one and a half years for this part, and we're only halfway through the strategy map.*
>
> *We did a gap analysis of where we are and where we want to be. "How do you get there?" is where the debate came in. We spent*

a month and a half discussing it. We're now strategy mapping by
department, but interdependent on other departments. Tactical
recommendations came from the strategy map. We get from it job
descriptions, deliverables, etc. It's a logical, sequential manage-
ment tool that fit the needs we had. The module is called priority
thinking. It's a long process, and there is no shortcut. I had been
wondering why my bright, well-intended senior managers could
not deliver on strategic execution.

The effect of implementing priority thinking at MasterCraft
was that the managers found themselves working much more collaboratively and working on areas they never seemed to be able to
get to. Dorton offers an example: "The day in the life of the VP
of sales used to consist of issues like 'We need a better guy in California, we need to get rid of the discounts, or whatever.' Now his
day is [devoted] to two main focuses: reduce our dependence on
wholesale push and increase retail pull to improve and control the
retail experience. He's now more focused."

That sales executive now spends time using internal IT systems
to analyze market data by geographic area so that when a dealer
says that his or her market does not need, say, a twenty-two-foot
Model X-30 wakeboard boat "because they don't sell here," the
MasterCraft VP can use his data to show what model and size are
appropriate for that market. The vice president can focus on
changing dealer behavior.

As MasterCraft's experience shows, there are distinct benefits of
forced collaboration:

- There is more delegation, as individuals focus on only what
  they should be focused on.
- Traffic control is better, since areas now interrelate more
  closely.
- People have a better sense of what they should be doing.

To assure that everyone did, in fact, collaborate, Dorton tied
compensation to the achievement of the strategic goals. "The tech-

nical staff wants to know what the bigger picture is. A requirement for successful forced collaboration is the free sharing of information." To assure that collaboration occurred all the way through the ranks, MasterCraft had the vision statement and core values printed on cards and requires all employees to always have the card with them. So any manager walking though the expansive manufacturing facility can stop any worker and ask to see the card. The cards became subtle reminders that everyone was required to collaborate to achieve common goals.

For example, before the forced-collaboration program was put into place, Rob May, director of marketing, used to create the marketing plan with an eye toward how it supported the brand. "Before we started this, we were disparate departments," says May. "We were successful despite ourselves."

"Now we look at growing the brand through collaboration," May says. "We now realize that every action should have a measurable result. In the past, we failed to leverage the relationships we had. This collaboration has forced us to say, 'What are we getting out of this relationship?' It used to be just gut feel. This is a deeper line of thinking. Now I look at how it drives sales. It also forces us to make difficult decisions and causes tough calls."

MasterCraft has traditionally sponsored many water sports events, professional athletes, and ski schools. Before forced collaboration, relationships with the athletes might not have been as close and not had any impact on sales. Now, with marketing closely tuned in to the needs of other departments and sharing a common understanding of business objectives, marketing measures its effectiveness based on sales. Says May:

> As the marketplace tightens, we have to ask the tough questions. It affects how we do the business. For me, it was a real spark. When I got here, we weren't really coordinated. I had been dealing with projects as they happened. I always wanted to be more strategic in my thinking. We do a lot of events and a lot of advertising. This new approach gives me a road map to what I want to accomplish.

Each time the departments get together, I learn more about each department's long-range plans. We used to talk about units we were moving. Now we focus on the big picture. We weren't doing this collectively. Now we're focused on accountability down to individuals. We give each person a road map. I now take time out of my daily schedule to think three years down the road. I used to think three days ahead. I actually talk to people in other departments, and we have a mutual understanding between departments and more of a kindred spirit.

CEO Dorton ties collaboration to communication: "At the end of the day, it's about sharing more information. Upper to middle management is the worst area in communication. Now the senior managers don't feel like they're spinning their wheels so much. It's a very new way of thinking for some because it's a challenge to the way they have always thought. But now one person can significantly impact the business, for the good or the bad."

Forced collaboration frees time for executives and managers all the way up the line, as more conflicts are resolved between departments or divisions. "For instance, I used to get the HR director coming to me to question the sales department, when he just passed the sales department office on the way to my office. Now they work this out with each other, which gives me more opportunity for free thought, and I can focus on more critical components of the business. I can be much more productive creating and communicating the vision."

The forced collaboration at MasterCraft requires that each person learn more of what the other departments are doing and their critical elements for their success. This approach helps link all the small successes to the greater strategic success of the business, as each department head becomes more aware of the impact of what he or she did on other departments. "This is a sound corporate philosophy that lets us focus on the critical, not the urgent," says Dorton. "This also allows me to speak to all personnel at all levels, since everyone now knows and relates to the strategic objectives and the tactics to get there."

Forcing collaboration not only makes managers work better together; its overall impact is to help an organization reach its potential.

Information Sharing

As MasterCraft learned and tough management requires, strong collaboration necessitates the sharing of information. While the information being shared in organizations today is relevant and useful, there could be more of it. While 22 percent of senior executives and managers say that the amount of information sharing at their organizations is extremely high, more than a third consider that information to be extremely relevant or useful to them. The smaller the company, the more information is shared, and the more relevant it is.

"I recently left a Fortune 200 company for a much smaller yet national organization," says a senior executive at a medium-sized company. "The focus of what is shared and why it is shared is so much clearer at the smaller company. It's remarkable."

There are two ways to look at information sharing in business. One is that increasing information sharing is a good thing, arming more people with more information to make better decisions. Another way to look at it is that information can get in the way of someone doing his or her job. The amount of information shared will always be debated as either not enough or too much. "In our organization, information is shared on a need-to-know basis," says a small-company manager. "Not all information is shared with all employees, only those involved. That way, only the people concerned can focus on the issue at hand and not have others trying to add to it."

SURVEY: INFORMATION SHARING

In general, the amount of information sharing at my organization is:

Extremely high	22%
Somewhat high	52%
Somewhat low	21%
Extremely low	5%

When it comes to the type and kind of information being shared in my organization, the majority of the information is:

Extremely relevant and/or useful to me	35%
Somewhat relevant and/or useful to me	58%
Somewhat irrelevant and/or useless to me	7%
Extremely irrelevant and/or useless to me	0%

In general, the amount of information sharing at my organization is:

	Senior Executives	Managers
Extremely high	25%	20%
Somewhat high	66%	43%
Somewhat low	6%	31%
Extremely low	3%	6%

Says another manager at a small company, "For some reason, those with valuable information to share like to keep it. Information that is shared is partial, sometimes irrelevant, and said quickly without an opportunity to ask questions. If this is the age of information, then we missed it. Truly great companies believe knowledge is power and empower the people to the fullest with as much information as they can possibly provide. But our company feels information clogs the system and we don't pay our people to think; we pay them to work."

In this age of transparency, it is easy to argue that sharing too much information is better than sharing not enough. However, the simple sharing of information does not mean anything positive will happen on the part of the recipient.

"Poor communication can result if I share too little, or if I throw so much at you it is overwhelming and meaningless," says Frank Ovaitt, president and CEO of the Institute for Public Relations, a nonprofit research and education organization funded by the industry.

Many executives perceive that sharing more information equates with better communications. "We have a client now that is building an international organization, and the issue is how do you reach all the employees and get the messages out," says Ovaitt. "The top people say there is no communication problem. They say they get a lot of e-mail, so they assume everyone else is, so communication is fine. No matter how many best practices about good communications there are out there, it's like every generation of managers has to learn it all over again."

With the sharing of information, two common problems can occur:

1. No action is requested or required by the executive or group sharing the information. Hence, nothing happens.
2. There is no obvious end benefit for anyone but the sender. That is, the recipient of the information has no reason to do anything about the information being shared.

To prevent these problems, before sharing information, you should take the first step of asking yourself, "Who has to do what for us to be successful?" The answer can help shape the communication. In Ovaitt's world, there are four steps for successful communication:

1. *Awareness.* By sharing the information, you at least help your target audience—employees or customers, for example—become aware of a situation or set of facts.
2. *Understanding.* Using logic, you can explain and reason through the information being shared. A constituency group can be made to clearly understand what's at stake.
3. *Readiness to do something.* The target group needs to be emotionally engaged or experience the issue themselves before they'll be ready to do something about it.
4. *The desired behavior.* You get the desired behavior by asking people to do something.

Tough management requires linking the information being shared to understanding, readiness, and finally action that will benefit the organization. "Often, we explain the information and maybe even the logic, but we never complete the process by asking the people to do something," says Ovaitt. "As a result, the behavior does not change. Sometimes, there's a sense that 'we need to get our story out there' on the part of executives, but they never think of the action." There are three potential actions for shared information:

1. Get somebody to do something.
2. Get somebody to stop something.
3. Allow someone else to do something.

But clearly, there will be no action unless you address the second communications challenge by giving the recipient a personal reason to do something based on the information. "If it isn't relevant to my job, my rewards, or my view of myself, why should I do it?" says Ovaitt. "Executives who are really naturals at communicating this way are few and far between. For most, it is something they have to learn to do." Information transparency builds greater trust, because it doesn't look like you're trying to hide anything, but you still need commitment and action. Companies often create a situation where it's clearly in the company's interest to have this information shared and action taken. But too often, it's not clear why it's in the individual's interest. What are the incentives to share?

Sometimes an organizational change can cause a shift in information sharing, either one way or the other. A new executive may have a more open view that more information shared can cause better decisions, while another might have the opposite view. No matter the view, the approach to the amount and type of information sharing—and whether it ever turns the corner from information to communication and action—starts from the top.

"Information sharing here changed when a major change at the executive level occurred. Up until that time it was nonexistent, irrelevant, and mostly inaccurate," says a senior executive at a medium-sized company.

"Because of top managers jockeying for position, information is a commodity used to attain advancement," says a manager at a small company. "Unfortunately, information is rarely provided unless the informer has something to gain."

Corporate culture and the attitudes of people who work in organizations play a great role in how much information is made available. Personalities also are a key. "We have one person who needs to know everything but is very selective in what is shared back," says a senior executive at a small company. "He probably failed kindergarten." Says a manager at a large company, "The amount of information I have from upper management is barely enough. This holding of information is deliberate. Upper management is engaged in turf warfare, and it seems that they consider information as weapons."

Interestingly, though many in business complain of information overload, the majority of executives and managers find the information they are receiving internally is useful and relevant. In today's work environment, with the potential for watercooler gossip and unproductive speculation, it is impossible to overcommunicate and share too much information. Correct information increases the effectiveness of communication, one of the most critical laws of tough management.

Top Characteristic Sought: Willingness to Learn

When you are practicing tough management, you are sharing and receiving information, communicating well, focusing on results and hard decisions, and by being flexible, being very open to learning new things. And if you happen to be looking for a new job in the future, you will have the top characteristic that an overwhelming majority (87 percent) of executives and managers would be looking for in new hires in the future. Only about half of executives and managers say that the majority of executives, managers, and employees in their organization today are willing to learn, though three-fourths say their current staff is knowledgeable about the business.

SURVEY: **WORKFORCE CHARACTERISTICS**

In my organization today, the majority of executives, managers, and employees, in general, share which of the following characteristics?

Knowledgeable about business	73%
Willing to learn	55%
Family oriented	53%
Trustworthy	45%
Loyal	43%
Balanced	42%
Conservative	41%
Technologically adept	41%
Willing to travel	40%
Aggressive	34%
Willing to change	34%
Knowledgeable about life	32%
Willing to share	30%
Willing to teach	27%
Open	25%
Fun	23%
Thankful/appreciative	22%

"As CEO and president of my own company, I share the philosophy of the founder of Mary Kay Cosmetics: priorities of God first, family second, and company third," says a senior executive at a small company. "It has worked for my company, and I support this view with my employees and subcontractors." Says a manager at a large company, "Current executives have blinders on to the real world. Balance and a willingness to learn and change will be critical success factors in the future."

When it comes to loyalty, only 43 percent say their current workforce is loyal, while 72 percent would seek loyalty in future hires. "Loyalty and knowledge will continue to be the single most important factors in acquiring new employees at the management level," says a manager at a medium-sized company. "Human equity is key. We will not only invest in capital improvements, such as technology and bricks and mortar, but in people, too."

When it comes to future hiring, loyalty is a more significant factor to senior executives than it is to managers. There obviously are differing viewpoints about characteristics, depending on the person's level in an organization. "It's difficult to group executives with the employee force," says a manager at a large company. "Employees have loyalty and a willingness to share and are knowledgeable. The executives are aggressive."

Interestingly, in both current and future workforces, the larger the company, the more aggressive is the management and employee base. Concerning trustworthiness, less than half of executives and managers say that characteristic was found in current managers and employees, but 87 percent would be looking for it in future employees. "We need to get back to demanding that we hire ethical, trustworthy, honest, conservative employees. That goes back to our core values," says a senior executive at a medium-sized company. "We must focus, focus, focus on our core values to be successful in our business and be loyal to our employees, customers, and shareholders. Overall, most of corporate America has lost this balance."

VOICES FROM THE FRONT LINES:
WORKFORCE CHARACTERISTICS

"Change is the only thing that's constant. Outsource, insource, acquisitions, merger, stabilize, repeat."

"The primary characteristic that I look for when hiring new employees is leadership capability. I want to make sure they understand themselves and their ability to serve, lead, and influence."

"People make or break an organization, and a key issue for a modern leader is sustainability. One can get short-term, but maybe not sustainable, results with very aggressive people and an 'end justifies the means' approach. Often this creates a difficult, less than fun environment. If we see a 'knowledge worker' shortage as the baby boom retires, the climate of the workplace will become critical to business results. Corporate cultures don't change quickly, so planning for the future must happen."

"It concerns me how conservative and fearful of sharing and learning top management has become. The best strategic plans will not help you if you have not created a culture of learning, improving, and (dare we say it) risk taking."

"What you measure and reward is what you get. Too many organizations expect balanced team-oriented performance but only reward stovepipe results."

"Over the past two years, we have had several rounds of layoffs that were the first for the company. As a result, the workforce has become much more conservative in its approach to business."

"When you speak of those in charge, there still are managers who are out for themselves and those who truly want to empower people who work for them. Hidden agendas still abound. Personal CYA can still come ahead of compassion, trust, or any other desired attributes. As we tighten the screws to stay competitive and the almighty bottom line rules, a growing survivalist mentality pervades the workplace. It keeps us competitive, but it is also eroding trust, sincerity, honesty, and respect."

When it comes to having executives, managers, and employees who are "fun," only 23 percent of respondents say their organization has them, while 38 percent look for that characteristic in future hiring. While more than half of management says their organization is staffed with people who are family oriented, only 40 percent would seek that characteristic in future hiring. So if you're planning a career move, tough management can serve you well, as you become more open and flexible in your ability to learn new ways, which is perceived to bring great benefit to the hiring organization.

Top Characteristics Desired in New Employees (in Order)
1. Willing to learn
2. Knowledgeable about the business
3. Trustworthy
4. Technologically adept
5. Balanced
6. Willing to change
7. Loyal
8. Willing to share
9. Willing to teach
10. Open
11. Knowledgeable about life
12. Family oriented
13. Fun

14. Thankful/appreciative

15. Willing to travel

The teamwork required for tough management also utilizes the great skill of communicating, as discussed in Chapter 1. Linking communication and forcing collaboration at all levels of the organization get more people organized on what matters most to the enterprise and, with flexibility, create an agile management that can move when required by the leadership.

CHAPTER 7

TOUGH MANAGEMENT WITHOUT BEING A TOUGH GUY

While the first six tenets of tough management deal with quantitative improvement, such as focusing on results, forcing hard decisions, and communicating crisply and clearly, the seventh deals with the qualitative aspects: improving your work life and that of the people around you. This can be done while still maintaining a tough—but fair—posture.

After all, tough management does not require treating subordinates brutally. On the contrary, business leaders should go out of their way to focus on the situations of those around them, with sympathy and understanding, and view their subordinates in a compassionate context. That is, the situations and motivations of the key subordinates—those who act in what they perceive to be the best interest of the business and strive to deliver—should be understood, taken into consideration, and leveraged to benefit both parties.

When it comes to understanding and appreciating how well subordinates do their work, business leaders could do much better. Only 10 percent of managers feel they are extremely well recognized for their work. Recognizing great work is one of the easiest responsibilities of leadership, yet the most poorly executed. Businesspeople are not just looking for the employee-of-the-month parking spot. In fact, the last things they want are trophies, awards, opportunities to present internally, or even time off. What they do want are bonuses for work performed, increased compensation, and a personal thank-you from their boss. The recognition and rewards they want are both financial and personal.

Time Spent at Work

Practicing tough management without appearing to be a cold-hearted beast takes an understanding of the situation of those being managed. For example, the number of hours executives and managers spend working is getting out of control. Not only has the myth of the eight-hour workday all but vanished, but the nine-hour day is falling by the wayside as well:

- Ninety-three percent of executives and managers are working nine or more hours per day.
- Seventy percent are working ten or more hours.
- For executives and managers, the forty-hour workweek is nonexistent, with 64 percent working more than fifty hours per week.

The challenge is for businesspeople to disconnect. The majority of executives and managers have ninety minutes or less of personal time during the workday. So the workday is getting longer, and businesspeople are taking less and less time during that workday, an unhealthy situation at best. "I do not know of anyone in our business who is not working harder, longer hours," says one senior executive at a large company.

The problem is not only the number of hours worked in the course of a day; it is the kind of hours worked. The pace of work is continuously increasing, with more meetings, decisions, and projects—and, consequently, more personal stress, as discussed in Chapter 4.

For many, this new work has become a way of life that, if left unchecked, can cause great unbalance within the managerial ranks. "A regular day for me is a ten-hour day," says Terry Sullivan, president of the Western Energy Institute, a regional and international trade association of energy companies, based in Portland, Oregon. Sullivan sees the "Internet pace" of business and increased focus

---

SURVEY: WORK TIME

On a typical workday, the number of hours I work (office, home, etc.) is about:

6 hours or less	0%
7 hours	1%
8 hours	5%
9 hours	23%
10 hours	41%
11 hours	17%
12 hours	10%
13 hours or more	3%

In a typical workweek, the number of hours I work (office, home, etc.) is:

Less than 30 hours	1%
30–40 hours	1%
41–50 hours	32%
51–60 hours	45%
61–70 hours	15%
71–80 hours	5%
81 or more hours	0%

on short-term results as the main culprits. "It's a hurry-up-and-get-things-done and do-it-with-less approach in business today," says Sullivan. "Somehow, we have to stop the madness or help ourselves and our staff develop the skills to manage effectively at this pace."

Businesspeople today need to get back to balance. For Sullivan, who has two children, ages five and seven, that means taking his children to the school bus on mornings that he is not traveling. Others find other ways to disconnect. Says one senior executive at a small company, "Although my sixty-hour workweeks have stayed the same over the years, the expectation of being able to work any-

---

VOICES FROM THE FRONT LINES: WORK TIME

"The demands of employers are exemplified by their cutting employees from the work field and adding additional work to the survivors. It is not necessarily all the better, more efficient workers that are left. Favoritism and lower salaries seem to be a solid reason to keep certain employees in certain positions."

"I am out of the office 80 percent of my workweek. If I added travel time, I would probably average sixty-one to seventy hours."

"The pace of work during the day, regardless of hours worked per day, is increasing almost continuously. More decisions, more meetings, more projects to keep track of, etc. Must be more productive, in part due to technology; however, it is more stressful."

"I have made a conscious decision and effort to better balance my work, family, and volunteer life."

---

time, anywhere is growing tiresome. The respect for evenings and weekends as personal time is dwindling with each passing year. I am struggling to disconnect on weekends and vacations more than ever."

"I have learned to simply not do certain things that have now become (in my view) nonessential," says a senior executive at a small company. "The good news is I am able to carve out some time for my family. The bad news is the quality of my performance has suffered, and the stress of not doing things to my satisfaction takes its toll. We can't be all things to all people and need to take back our lives. I'm doing this one hour at a time."

Working more is sometimes mistaken for doing good work. "I am convinced there is much confusion about what doing a good job actually is," says a manager at a large company. "Long hours are not it. Quality of work done, working on the correct things are more important than long hours. The long hours, rush, rush, rush culture comes from above from deluded individuals."

The key in tough management is to understand that everyone is in the same situation. The people you are managing and those managing you all are working at the same feverish pace. You have to force yourself as well as those around you to pause and take a break; otherwise, you all will lose perspective.

Workload Increasing Faster than Compensation

It's not just time put in at work that causes stress; it is the actual workload that you and your colleagues face during that time. The majority of executives and managers have seen the amount of work they do and their responsibilities increase significantly compared with a few years ago. But during that same time period, only 10 percent have seen their total compensation increase significantly.

Workload has increased significantly more in the largest companies, those with more than ten thousand employees. Meanwhile,

---

SURVEY: WORKLOAD

Compared with two years ago, the amount of work (number of hours, responsibilities, results, etc.) I do today has:

Increased significantly	46%
Increased somewhat	34%
Stayed the same	13%
Decreased somewhat	6%
Decreased significantly	2%

Compared with two years ago, my total compensation (salary, bonuses, stock options, etc.) has:

Increased significantly	10%
Increased somewhat	52%
Stayed the same	23%
Decreased somewhat	12%
Decreased significantly	4%

---

compensation has increased significantly mostly in companies with fewer than five hundred employees.

Economic pressures of the past few years have caused many organizations to trim staff while at least maintaining, if not increasing, production. This has left workers at all levels with more to do. "Doing more with less is becoming both figurative and now literal, even among senior-executive ranks," says a senior executive at a large company. Says a manager at a medium-sized company, "The company wants us to accomplish more e-business initiatives, but with the same amount of people. I end up doing more and more of the administrative, number-crunching, and training-of-users roles, since we have no resources to pick those up."

In many cases, corporate downsizing has forced an increased work burden on the best and the brightest in the workforce. "The price of showing competence is increasing responsibility and work," complains a manager at a small company. The fundamental problem with this situation is that it can be a short-term situation, at best. Executives and managers cannot effectively function on a high-speed treadmill for extended periods of time. Judgments suffer, and by trying to do too much, an organization risks mistakes. "Things could not be more intense," says a senior executive at a medium-sized company. "It's impossible to keep track of all the work, and it's growing exponentially."

In addition to working more hours, managers and executives experience greater personal pressure because of added duties. "I have more responsibility, my decisions have more of an impact on the bottom line, but it does not necessarily take up more of my time," says one manager at a medium-sized company. "The number of hours is not necessarily commensurate with responsibility level."

Tough management requires that leaders take the time to check if those who have taken on additional work over the past few years are being fairly compensated for that work, which is not always the case. "In the quest for continual improvement and increased productivity, much of the human center has been removed from business," says a senior executive at a large company. "Our energies are devoted to an ever-increasing set of demands while we fail to nurture the most basic strategic advantage of any company, our employees. It is time to return to leadership rather than reactive management."

The impact on businesses of not keeping compensation in line with workload can be felt on a company's biggest asset, its employees. "It has become an all-too-familiar trend: take on more work, have your pay cut by a percentage in order to keep the company in business and have a job," says one manager at a small company.

"A large number of people in the workforce are rapidly reaching burnout."

Taking Personal Time

Tough management requires that you take more personal time during the workday. Because of the increasing workload, senior executives and managers find themselves spending more time at the office, with most of that time being spent on work. Almost four-fifths of senior executives and managers have ninety minutes or less of personal time on a typical workday. The majority have sixty minutes or less. Of the workday time that is considered "personal," the majority spend it eating meals. Fewer than one-third spend it exercising, and one-fifth spend it reading or thinking.

All work with no break can be unhealthy not only for the individual but for the business as well. When businesspeople always have their heads down, there is less time for thinking and maintaining perspective. Decision making can become clouded, as decisions get made just for expediency, so everyone can get back to work.

SURVEY: PERSONAL TIME

In a typical workday, how much personal time (nonwork: errands, meals, etc.) do you have?

None	6%
1–30 minutes	24%
31–60 minutes	32%
61–90 minutes	17%
1.5–2 hours	5%
2–3 hours	5%
3–4 hours	8%
More than 4 hours	4%

Tough management requires that businesses realize their people need a break. While economic conditions have caused a reduction in the number of workers, the workload has fallen on those who remain, causing constant work with no break. This can lead to resentment within the workforce, which can lead to instability, especially as economic conditions improve and those feeling they have been oppressed seek greener pastures in other companies. States one manager, "Executive management endorses overload and stress by not addressing the stress levels even when things have seemingly turned around with business. It makes you think that workers are much like used napkins; use them until they aren't too good, and then discard them and get another to replace it."

Ways to Break Away from Work

Here are a few ways you can change focus from the daily grind at work. Just taking a short time away to let your mind and body recharge can increase productivity when back to the office.

- *Take a two-hour lunch.* Get away for more than a sandwich at the desk.
- *Go home early one day.* Pick a day, any day, and leave early, and don't contact the office again until the next day. When it comes to work-life balance, 68 percent of executives and managers believe businesspeople are unbalanced.
- *Think.* With so many fires to put out and tasks to accomplish, there's no free time to think anymore. Take the time, clear your head, and then get back to work. Companies need clear thinkers.
- *Exercise.* Even if it's just a walk around the block, get away from the office and be physical.
- *Read.* Pick something that isn't work-related. Get away from the work mentally.

"I spend a few minutes a day catching up on the news, the intent being business-related news, but invariably get drawn into the occasional non-work-related article."

"I spend a lot of personal time dreaming/visioning, which to me is a little more than thinking, because it helps me create a vision of my goals—business and personal. I envision how I am going to make a board presentation as well as mentally plotting a vacation."

"I rarely have personal time while at work except for time allocated for lunch. I do, however, occasionally have meetings during work hours for civic volunteer work that we are encouraged to participate in."

"My organization requires its managers to fulfill job duties rather than hours in a day. On some days I may choose to spend ten hours working feverishly on a work-related project, and on others I may have the luxury of coming in late, dawdling on personal e-mail, and leaving early. As long as I perform excellently, I have great latitude in how I spend my time."

"Based on my work habits, basically no personal time. Rare lunches, exercise. Bad habits are hard to change."

"Busy schedules have made eating lunch at your desk a frequent occurrence."

"Due to having to serve in three roles at one time, my typical workday is full of meetings and staying late to do work and taking it home. All weekends consist of some form of work from a couple hours to twenty-plus. I used to exercise, but lately I haven't had time before work, at lunch, or after work—leading to my putting on weight and not feeling very healthy! It hasn't been fun lately!"

The healthy organization of tomorrow has to realize today how hard the people who work for them are working, at all levels. For many companies, the past few years have been very trying, and managers see morale as significantly decreased from two years ago. Taking more breaks from work may not change the work or workload, but it can improve the attitude of those charged with doing it.

Top Uses of Personal Time During the Workday (in Order)
1. Meals
2. Personal errands
3. Internet browsing
4. Family matters
5. Exercise
6. Reading
7. Thinking
8. Medical appointments
9. Watching television
10. Shopping

The Business Case for Golf

Including equipment, green fees, and tourism, the U.S. golf economy is worth $62 billion, according to the World Golf Foundation, which has determined that there are 36.7 million golf participants in the United States. (There were 502 million rounds of golf played in one year.) Everyone knows that much of the golf played by businesspeople is either during weekends, on holidays, or on an occasional official business golf outing, where clients or business partners might be included.

The reality is that there is greatly unproductive time during the workday where a few-hour break would hardly be missed:

- Businesspeople say they are most productive before 9:00 A.M. and after 5:00 P.M.
- Over half (61 percent) of executives and managers are most productive between 7:00 A.M. and 9:00 A.M.
- Eighteen percent are most productive before 7:00 A.M.
- The second-highest productivity times are after 5:00 P.M., with 33 percent most productive between 5:00 P.M. and 8:00 P.M. and 12 percent most productive after 8:00 P.M.

The two most often cited peak-productivity times are before and after traditional work hours, with all top choices falling outside the traditional hours. As the official workday starts at 9:00 A.M., productivity begins to drop:

- Thirty-five percent are productive between 9:00 A.M. and 11:00 A.M., before personal productivity falls through the floor.
- Only 9 percent say they feel productive in terms of work completed between 11:00 A.M. and 2:00 P.M., and only 11 percent are productive between 2:00 P.M. and 5:00 P.M.

This means that from the standpoint of work productivity, the best time to play golf during the workweek is starting at 11:00 A.M., and the second-best tee time would be 2:00 P.M., as long as you can get back to the office by 5:00 P.M., when personal productivity starts to ramp up again.

Midday productivity drops because of interruptions from subordinates, peers, managers, and the "fire of the day" to be put out. The result is that much of the work time during the day is spent reacting, not acting. The events drive the direction of the individual, and the daily tasks that the individual intended to complete have to be put on hold until later in the day or even pushed to the next day, when people come in early to be productive before the next daily rush.

So much time is spent reacting that there is little time left for businesspeople to think. This is where golf comes in. Since 11:00

A.M. to 2:00 P.M. is the least productive time for many, why not spend it on the golf course, thinking?

It could be good for the economy, perhaps increasing the $871.37 spent per golfer. People at the office who could not turn to you for a solution to their crisis of the moment would have to become more creative in solving issues on their own. This would increase creativity on their part, and productivity as well.

Seriously, taking a break in the course of a day or a week is critical to the bottom line of the organization. It creates a better frame of mind for making better decisions and lets managers and executives get better focused on results that matter, which is key to tough management.

Employee Morale

Part of the fallout of so much time spent working is a decline in the mood of the workforce. Economic conditions over the last few years also have taken their toll on the workforce, as both senior executives and managers acknowledge a significant drop in employee morale at their organizations over that period. Three-quarters of senior executives and managers rated overall employee morale in their organizations as either extremely or somewhat high versus what they said concerning two years previously. Today, only half of these same respondents say that morale at their organizations is high.

A number of factors play into the decline in morale, many of them having to do with economic conditions. "Time, increased workloads, and economic conditions are eroding employee confidence and morale," says a manager at a large company. "People are more concerned about losing their jobs and family security." Employees today face job insecurity, head count reductions, and a leveling off of pay. It's tough for workers to stay motivated with discussions of pending or potential layoffs swirling all around the office.

SURVEY: EMPLOYEE MORALE

Overall employee morale at my organization today is:

Extremely high	10%
Somewhat high	43%
Somewhat low	39%
Extremely low	8%

Overall employee morale at my organization two years ago was:

Extremely high	19%
Somewhat high	56%
Somewhat low	20%
Extremely low	5%

Morale problems sometimes are caused at the leadership level of a business. With the high turnover rate of top executives these days comes increased anxiety and lower morale. And the leaders who are not leaving are under increased pressure to deliver improving results in difficult times. "Morale is slipping because the organization's leadership is once again slashing costs to improve margins," says a manager at a medium-sized company. "Unfortunately, this leadership is lacking both the vision and the intelligence to grow the business. So it's cut, cut, cut. They reduce the benefits and salaries of the folks who work ten- to twelve-hour days and truly care about their jobs and the corporation, while their benefits and pay keep rising at obnoxious levels."

Additional anxiety is created by an increasing lack of loyalty, with the feeling that if business hits a downturn, no one in the company is safe. As a result, many are working harder to sock away whatever they can. Says a manager at a large company, "With focus

"My organization is having an excellent financial year, so most employees are excited. On the downside, because there is very little loyalty in either direction, it's in the back of everyone's mind that if things go bad, no one is safe."

"Current threatened layoffs make employee morale low."

"We worked hard on improvement projects a few years ago. As a result, we had some inertia to move forward. Since the recession hit, that has all died. Now there are not enough people to work on new projects. Everyone is so stretched, changing the goal to maintaining the status quo."

"I work for a state institution. Budgets have just been slashed, pay increases are not even mentioned, and classified service contracts are way behind and further delayed by legislators. It's hard to say why employees would feel any kind of optimism. Those of us responsible to keep operations going need to focus on nonmonetary rewards of working together and serving the needs of our stakeholders."

"Economic turnaround (negative) has created nonproductive management. Economic fraud has created high governance and lowered creativity. Creative management has been pushed out of [our] organization to make place for governance and red tape."

"A Tale of Two Companies: In all 'mergers of equals,' one partner always seems to come out on top, more equal. We've completed just such a merger. Two CEOs, one leaves, the other wins. The subsequent reorganization will benefit the operating company of the remaining CEO. Most of the jobs and promotions are taking place in that city.

The other company is gutted of its management and profits. How's the employee morale?"

"After coping with reduction in benefits, frozen wages, reduced head count, it would be hard for any company to maintain or promote any type of morale boost. To be sure, I'm confident that some companies have found a way to make this all work. Unfortunately, my company is not one of them. With all the uncertainty in the telecom sector, I'm sure many people are here because there are so few other opportunities. It seems every week that someone gets the feeling that it is better to be unemployed than continue to fight."

"New executive leadership and emphasis on communication has had great effect on employee morale in this organization."

"The economic stress and market/life conditions have made all of us a bit more hesitant."

on financial performance being forced to a thirty-day window, most of the sales teams are not willing to take vacation or downtime for fear of missing a commission."

There are huge downsides to low morale in a business. Unhappy employees are not as productive, and they don't have the incentive to be creative to move the organization forward. There also is potential risk to the business itself.

"There is strong linkage between morale, security, and corporate liability," says MacDonnell Ulsch, Managing Director of Janus Risk Management. "Most security breaches originate inside the organization, and the breach may be the direct action of a disgruntled employee, or a disgruntled employee may assist someone outside in violating the integrity of the company."

Tough management requires that top executives take steps to assure that low employee morale is not hurting their business, thereby decreasing value to shareholders. The first step for an organization is to identify its current employee morale level. For example, senior executives have a dramatically higher perception of employee morale in their organizations than do the managers, who are closer to the employees. "If morale is suffering, the senior management is the last to know," says a senior executive at a small company.

Top executives need to listen more to employees, candidly, and institute processes to continually benchmark morale levels, which can present somewhat of a challenge. Executives also need to communicate more, or at least better, as detailed in Chapter 1.

At the personal level, managers and employees must keep balanced to improve their own morale, sometimes looking outside the job for that personal satisfaction. "My job morale is not too hot, but I keep my spirits up by doing other things, writing and teaching, which make life a bit more interesting," says the CIO of one major organization. Higher employee morale means lower turnover, less training, and more familiarity with the company, its products, and its customers. And when the economy and business pick up, these employees are more likely to stay where they are happy.

Death of Ambition

Another context that you have to keep in mind for tough management is that the extreme, personal ambition of the late 1990s has dropped significantly as businesspeople reevaluate what's important to them. Triggered by the events of September 11, 2001, a few years of harsh economic forces in business, and family pressures, executives and managers are recalibrating the intensity of their drive.

SURVEY: AMBITION

When it comes to ambition in your professional (work) life, how ambitious do you feel today?

Extremely	40%
Somewhat	51%
Not very	9%
Not at all	0%

When it comes to ambition in your professional (work) life, how ambitious did you feel two years ago?

Extremely	69%
Somewhat	28%
Not very	2%
Not at all	0%

A few years ago, 69 percent of executives and managers considered themselves extremely ambitious in their professional lives. Today, only 40 percent consider themselves extremely ambitious. This is a fundamental shift in attitude, which could have a profound effect on business, as people begin to balance their lives more holistically, bringing a different perspective to the workplace.

Though the reasons vary, many say they are reallocating their time and energy on what matters to them now. "A few years back, my drive was very high," says one manager. "I'm not sure if it's burnout, family commitments, satisfaction with my current position, or being near the top of the ladder that has slowed the ambition level, but it definitely is not what it used to be."

"In the last two years I have been marginalized to the point that I have lost any ambition for my present job," says one manager. Says the fifty-six-year-old CEO of a small company, "The recession makes me feel like a boxer who knows he's losing in the twelfth round." Says another manager, "The decline of ambition is less the wisdom of age and diminishment of expectations than it is weariness of the battle both within the firm and in the face of external forces."

Another consistent theme is internal company politics. "I have become disillusioned with my role in corporate America; too much politics and not enough reward for value given," says one manager at a large company. Another says, "My ambition is now tempered by the increased level of stress, chaos, and uncertainty in the workplace." A manager at a large company reflects, "Having a child took a lot of the drive out of my ambition. It opened my eyes to what is truly important in my life. Those above me work 24/7, and the politics are fierce. I don't find the game attractive anymore. I get more satisfaction out of *Green Eggs and Ham*."

The irony is that a dramatic decrease in work ambition can actually improve business. Executives and managers who better balance their work and family life will bring to their job a healthier and broader perspective. A personally balanced view from the top also can trickle down to the troops the idea that a more balanced life is OK.

Efficiency can increase, as managers push more for project execution so they can get home sooner. "As my kids get older, I am more willing to prioritize my projects at work to spend time with them," says one manager.

This reprioritization of work and home life, coupled with the death of the extreme work ambition of the past, will give birth to a new kind of ambition. Rather than the intense, self-centered ambition of the late nineties, there will be new, balanced leaders with a more external viewpoint.

Protecting the Talent

Besides addressing declining morale and less-intense ambition, tough management requires a continuous evaluation of whether and how the best employees, managers, and executives are being rewarded. The world of work has changed, and there are no signs that it will ever go back to the way it was, say, a decade ago. Organizations are going to be dealing with a host of new management issues in the coming months and years.

If businesses don't take positive action, two primary issues can cause a talent drain. First, business leaders are optimistic about their business futures, with many planning to increase the number of employees in the future. Second, employee morale has dropped significantly from past levels, and many managers feel overworked and undervalued. This changes loyalty, on the part of both employers and employees, as described earlier.

But another factor in morale is the sheer workload that many have had to assume during the corporate belt-tightening of the past few years. With the disappearance of the forty-hour workweek and the shrinking of personal time, managers find themselves working at home and on nights and weekends.

The issue of working remotely is different from the issue of working more. The majority of businesspeople say that working remotely has made their lives better, but it does not address the burden of workload. It is that extra workload that upsets many. While many companies either downsized or kept workforces steady, the amount of work increased. Many of the best in an organization's talent pool were called upon to take on the extra load.

The economy played a significant role in driving this, as more companies competed for less business. Each sale became more difficult, and every dollar to the bottom line became harder to earn. While managers might intellectually understand and appreciate this external force as the cause, it doesn't change the amount of work they have had to assume.

As business comes back, the attitude of these individuals could change. During difficult times, fear of losing a job can drive day-to-day attitudes and actions. As business and the economy improve, opportunities and the prospects of greener pastures could drive those attitudes and actions. Tough management requires that the leaders of departments and organizations take steps now to protect their talent pool. The leadership should step up and clearly communicate to those below not just the game plan for the future of the business, but also the plan for the future of the people who held that business together during tough times.

Recognize Someone for Doing a Good Job

To practice tough management without appearing too tough requires that you recognize those around you for a job well done. When it comes to being well recognized by their superiors for understanding and appreciating their work, the superiors get a poor rating. And if you work in a very large company, you are likely to be very disappointed when it comes to recognition. In companies with more than ten thousand employees, virtually no one says they are extremely well recognized. Those who are the most acknowledged are in companies with fewer than five hundred employees. There also are some differences between what senior executives and managers would prefer:

- Less than a third of top executives want to be recognized by an increase in responsibility.
- Almost half of managers want more responsibility.
- Significantly more managers than executives want a promotion as well as opportunities to attend external events and recognition at company events.

Sometimes, words from above can provide a true sense of being appreciated. "I've always appreciated it when my boss sends a note to the other executives mentioning my success," says one manager at a medium-sized company. At a large company, a manager says,

SURVEY: JOB RECOGNITION

When it comes to your superiors recognizing (understanding and appreciating) your work, how well are you recognized?

Extremely well	14%
Somewhat well	51%
Not very well	27%
Not at all well	8%

When it comes to your superiors recognizing (understanding and appreciating) your work, how well are you recognized?

	Senior Executives	Managers
Extremely well	16%	12%
Somewhat well	45%	54%
Not very well	30%	25%
Not at all well	7%	8%

When it comes to appreciation for your work, how would you prefer to be recognized?

Senior Executives

Bonus	70%
Increased compensation	64%
Personal thank-you	52%
Increased responsibility	30%
Promotion	21%
E-mail from superior	18%
Personal note from superior	18%
Recognition at company event	16%
Time off	15%
Phone call from superior	12%
Inclusion in more meetings	11%
Opportunity to attend external event(s)	11%

Opportunity to present internally	8%
Trophy, certificate, award, etc.	1%

Managers

Increased compensation	74%
Bonus	71%
Increased responsibility	48%
Personal thank-you	48%
Promotion	38%
Opportunity to attend external event(s)	31%
E-mail from superior	30%
Recognition at company event	30%
Personal note from superior	27%
Inclusion in more meetings	25%
Time off	18%
Phone call from superior	16%
Opportunity to present internally	15%
Trophy, certificate, award, etc.	12%

When it comes to your superiors recognizing (understanding and appreciating) your work, how well are you recognized?

	Small (1–499)	Medium (500–9,999)	Large (10,000+)
Extremely well	25%	13%	0%
Somewhat well	42%	44%	67%
Not very well	23%	33%	26%
Not at all well	8%	8%	7%

"Just knowing you are on the right track because you receive positive feedback is often reward enough. Other rewards would be nice, but contributing and being of value to the company has better long-term impact."

"Senior management at my company expects all managers to recognize employees for their efforts. A system was put in place at my company to make recognition easy for managers, allowing them to select gifts from a Web-based system. My manager has approached me numerous times to make sure I am recognizing my direct and indirect reports for performing above and beyond."

"My manager is excellent about recognizing individuals and teams for contributions on a regular basis; however, there is very little if any way to monetarily compensate for going above and beyond."

"Sometimes not only is personal recognition a good thing, teamwork recognition has a multiplier effect in leaders of teams."

"It is not the reward (money, time, or attention), it's the real interest in what my company (as part of a bigger group of companies) is doing and what my colleagues are doing with what result."

"Public recognition and thank-yous should be given to the team I am responsible for—they helped cause the success."

And those words don't necessarily have to be directly to the manager, as a senior executive at a small company points out: "Probably the most rewarding and memorable are the sincerely kind words. The most impact in my forty-seven years was the CEO who sent a letter to my adolescent daughters, explaining to them the significance of an industry award I had received."

People in business want to be valued and respected. If you can't increase compensation or distribute a bonus, it is necessary to go out of your way to compliment one of your managers or employees who has been doing a good job.

Top Ten Ways People Want to Be Recognized for Their Work (in Order)

1. Bonus
2. Increased compensation
3. Personal thank-you
4. Increased responsibility
5. Promotion
6. E-mail from superior
7. Recognition at company event
8. Personal note from superior
9. Opportunity to attend external event
10. Inclusion in more meetings

Sources for Doing Your Job Better

Another way to improve morale and protect the talent is to provide ways for people to do their jobs better. Tough management means addressing this qualitative side of executives, managers, and employees by providing tools to help individuals improve practical things they do, as well as those that inspire and motivate them. The sources where businesspeople get the most practical tips, guidance, and tactics to do their jobs better are attending conferences and seminars. Next most important are spending more time on networking and interpersonal relations. These sources are where most business executives and managers today are getting their best guidance and ideas to help them do their jobs better.

- The other best sources for practical tips cited are, in order, networking and interpersonal relations, personal experience, books, online research, peers, newsletters and periodicals, industry experts, mentors, and industry trade magazines.
- The sources from which the fewest executives and managers say they receive the best tips are, in order, television and radio, family, friends, meetings, their boss, and their subordinates.

SURVEY: BUSINESS SOURCES

The sources where I get the most practical tips, guidance, and tactics to do my job better are:

Conferences/seminars	74%
Networking and interpersonal relations	60%
Personal experience	59%
Books	57%
Online research	50%
Peers	48%
Newsletters, periodicals, etc.	42%
Industry experts	40%
Mentors	36%
Industry trade magazines	35%
Subordinates	31%
My boss	28%
Meetings	24%
Friends	24%
Family	13%
TV/radio	7%

When it comes to getting inspiration and motivation to help them do their jobs better, executives and managers also rank conferences and seminars as number one. The other sources of inspiration and motivation are, in order, books, networking and interpersonal relations, family, personal experience, mentors, friends, peers, and their boss. The sources that the fewest cite as their best sources of inspiration and motivation are, in order, television and radio, industry and trade magazines, meetings, online research, newsletters and periodicals, subordinates, and industry experts.

While conferences and seminars are the first choice both for practical tips and motivation, more managers than senior executives selected these as the best sources of practical tips or of inspiration and motivation. More managers than senior executives also see reading books and online research as the best sources of guidance for performing their jobs better.

The choice of conferences, seminars, and reading books indicates that in the consumer-focused business environment of today, more executives and managers should be focused externally. Conferences and seminars often allow attendees to mingle with their peers in other companies or even industries and to hear market-related information from speakers. They also provide an opportunity to increase networking within an industry, association, or peer

---

VOICES FROM THE FRONT LINES: BUSINESS SOURCES

"Regularly listen to motivational tapes and read self-development material."

"Inspiration, coping, and advancement come most strongly from continually improving skills as a servant leader."

"Like life, one's career is also a journey. Take advantage of the moments along the way. They cannot be planned, but one can certainly take advantage of the inspirational and educational pause."

"A former boss once told me, 'If you need to read a book to get motivated, then you don't have what it takes to succeed at a high level.'"

"Reading and networking are where I get the most practical and inspirational advice and guidance."

---

group. These networking opportunities can be beneficial corporately as well as personally.

The business benefits when its executives and managers have a more outwardly focused and market-based background that is current. Too often, people inside companies spend an excessive amount of time meeting with and talking to people inside their own companies. This creates a risk of market insulation.

In addition to the obvious exercise of spending more time with customers, executives and managers should spend more time outside their immediate area internally, and outside their specific company area externally.

Moving outside of your office area can be a healthy eye-opener. "The best place for true enlightenment and motivation is the shop floor," says one manager at a medium-sized company. A senior executive at a small company learns from employees served by the executive's department and from customers: "I get the best motivation and ideas for doing my job better from my customers, both internal and external."

The personal benefits of attending external events such as conferences include more time for clear thinking. "Sometimes you need some quiet time for your mind so that creative ideas can emerge and develop," says a senior executive at a small company. "Giving your mind some space enables this most powerful tool. It can then draw upon past knowledge and experience without being cluttered with day-to-day business drama."

Though spreadsheets and business plans are essential for the business to operate, it is the interactions with people on the outside that can provide a better knowledge base from which to create those spreadsheets and plans. Current market knowledge can provide individuals and their companies with a more reality-based approach to conducting business. (Plus, many of those external conferences are much more interesting than those repetitive internal meetings with the same people!) Tough management requires this external focus so that the results that are sought are on target.

Top Ten Sources for Inspiration/Motivation to Do a Better Job (in Order)

1. Conferences/seminars
2. Books
3. Networking and interpersonal relations
4. Family
5. Personal experience
6. Mentors
7. Friends
8. Peers
9. B`oss
10. Industry experts

Just Say Thanks

One of the best ways to practice tough management without being a tough guy is to stop what you're doing, look around your group or department or company, and identify someone who needs and deserves a pat on the back. With business going so fast and everyone so busy, at every level, there often is little time to think about being thankful for what is at work, or to take time to say "thank-you" to someone else. Executives, managers, and employees who are working ten-plus hours a day with less than an hour of free time might feel hard-pressed to feel thankful for anything to do with work.

Many can be thankful for still having a job, considering the millions who have lost their jobs due to downsizing over the past few years. You can be thankful that the majority of companies plan to increase their number of employees over the next year.

You might thank your superiors for that promotion or raise, or thank them for not promoting you, since you are stressed enough already.

Thank a customer, whether business-to-business or consumer, for buying your product or service. Without customers, there is no business.

Thank your family for understanding or at least appreciating how hard you work when you are not at home. And thank your spouse or family for working so hard at home while you're at the office. Neither is necessarily easy.

Thank someone for providing you with good customer service, whether on the phone or in person. Those who provide customer service deal with too many irate customers who can be the opposite of thankful. Customer service agents often take much abuse.

Thank whoever at your company allows you to work at home at times. Thank the person who copied you on that e-mail (and also thank the person who did not copy you on that useless one).

Thank the person who made the meeting run smoothly, and especially thank the one who made it start on time. Thank whoever is responsible for canceling that recurring, useless meeting you always had to attend.

Thank all the people who worked long hours to get that report or project done, so you could be more effective at a meeting or even get some much-needed sleep.

Thank the assistants and secretaries, who everyone knows really make the business work.

Thank the person who actually calls you back, and thank someone for actually answering the phone.

Thank the chief executive who clearly articulated the company's strategy and direction. And if you are the chief executive, thank all those below you who have to execute that strategy.

Thank the person who gave you the heads-up about something at work that you needed to know but no one else told you.

Thank someone in your technology department for working extremely hard to make things work with limited budgets. Thank someone in your financial department for keeping your business straight and making sure you and your associates always get paid.

If your stock is going up, thank your stockholders. If it's going down, be thankful you don't have to sell right now.

Thank your boss for the autonomy and challenges, and thank your managers and employees for rising to the challenges you provide.

Thank the executive, manager, or employee for telling you the truth, even if it was bad news.

There are many other things to be thankful for at work, so in the course of a day, go out of your way to say thanks to someone. If everyone did this, there would be a more appreciative office environment.

Thanks for taking the time to read about tough management and to think about practicing it.

INDEX